Great Meals in Minutes was created by Rebus, Inc. and published by Time-Life Books.

Rebus, Inc.

Publisher: Rodney Friedman
Editorial Director: Shirley Tomkievicz

Editor: Marya Dalrymple
Art Director: Ronald Gross
Managing Editor: Brenda Goldberg
Senior Editor: Cara De Silva
Food Editor and Food Stylist: Grace Young
Photographer: Steven Mays
Prop Stylist: Cathryn Schwing
Staff Writer: Alexandra Greeley
Associate Editor: Ann Harvey
Assistant Editor: Bonnie J. Slotnick
Assistant Food Stylist: Nancy Leland Thompson
Recipe Tester: Gina Palombi Barclay
Production Assistant: Lorna Bieber

For information about any Time-Life book, please write:
Reader Information
Time-Life Books
541 North Fairbanks Court
Chicago, Illinois 60611

Library of Congress Cataloging in Publication Data
French regional menus.
　　(Great meals in minutes)
　　Includes index.
　　1. Cookery, French.　2. Menus.
　　3. Cooks—Biography.
I. Time-Life Books.　II. Series.
TX719.F83　1984　　641.5944　84-8868
ISBN 0-86706-190-1 (retail ed.)
ISBN 0-86706-191-X (lib. bdg.)

Time-Life Books Inc.
is a wholly owned subsidiary of
Time Incorporated

Founder: Henry R. Luce 1898–1967
Editor-in-Chief: Henry Anatole Grunwald
President: J. Richard Munro
Chairman of the Board: Ralph P. Davidson
Corporate Editor: Jason McManus
Group Vice President, Books: Joan D. Manley

Time-Life Books Inc.

Editor: George Constable
Executive Editor: George Daniels
Director of Design: Louis Klein
Board of Editors: Dale M. Brown, Thomas A. Lewis, Robert G. Mason, Ellen Phillips, Peter Pocock, Gerry Schremp, Gerald Simons, Rosalind Stubenberg, Kit van Tulleken, Henry Woodhead
Director of Administration: David L. Harrison
Director of Research: Carolyn L. Sackett
Director of Photography: John Conrad Weiser

President: Reginald K. Brack Jr.
Senior Vice President: William Henry
Vice Presidents: George Artandi, Stephen L. Bair, Robert A. Ellis, Juanita T. James, Christopher T. Linen, James L. Mercer, Joanne A. Pello, Paul R. Stewart

Editorial Operations
Design: Anne B. Landry (art coordinator); James J. Cox (quality control)
Research: Phyllis K. Wise (assistant director), Louise D. Forstall
Copy Room: Diane Ullius
Production: Celia Beattie, Gordon E. Buck,
Correspondent: Miriam Hsia (New York)

SERIES CONSULTANT
Margaret E. Happel is the author of *Ladies Home Journal Adventures in Cooking*, *Ladies Home Journal Handbook of Holiday Cuisine*, and other best-selling cookbooks, as well as the translator and adapter of Rebecca Hsu Hiu Min's *Delights of Chinese Cooking*. A food consultant based in New York City, she has been director of the food department of *Good Housekeeping* and editor of *American Home* magazine.

WINE CONSULTANT
Tom Maresca combines a full-time career teaching English literature with writing about and consuming fine wines. He is now at work on *The Wine Case Book*, which explains the techniques of wine tasting.

Cover: Jill Van Cleave and William Rice's chicken with garlic-vinegar sauce, Lyonnaise salad, and chocolate pots de crème with chestnuts. See pages 78–80.

Great Meals
IN MINUTES

FRENCH REGIONAL
MENUS

TIME-LIFE BOOKS, ALEXANDRIA, VIRGINIA

Contents

Meet the Cooks

CAROL BRENDLINGER AND MICHAEL WILD

What started out as a hobby for Carol Brendlinger, who grew up in Pennsylvania, and Michael Wild, who was born in France, has become a profession and a way of life for them both. Today they are chefs for the Bay Wolf Restaurant and Cafe in Oakland, California. Besides cooking, Michael Wild selects the wine for the restaurant, and Carol Brendlinger teaches cooking classes and develops recipes for numerous publications.

JEANNE VOLTZ

New Yorker Jeanne Voltz, a six-time winner of the Vesta Award for newspaper food writing and editing, has been the food editor of *The Miami Herald* and *The Los Angeles Times*. She was also the food editor of *Woman's Day* magazine and is the author of five cookbooks, including *The California Cookbook*. She is a founding member of the New York City chapter of Les Dames d'Escoffier and a member of La Chaine de Rôtisseurs, both gastronomic societies.

LESLEE REIS

Until Leslee Reis married, she had never cooked an entire meal. Today she is the owner and head chef of Café Provençal in Evanston, Illinois, and a partner in Leslee's, a casual restaurant in the same city that features eclectic American meals. She has worked as a caterer, a restaurant consultant, and a teacher of French cooking, and has been cited by the media numerous times for her contributions to the food profession.

JACQUES MOKRANI

Jacques Mokrani, who was raised in Algiers, attended the hotel and restaurant school of the Société Hôtelière in Marseilles, France. Later, he served as an apprentice at the Savoy Grill in London and gained further experience as a *chef de partie* for the French Line. In 1973, he opened his own restaurant, LaBoucane, in San Francisco, and then in 1979 moved it to the city of Napa, in the heart of California wine country.

JOHN CASE

Raised in Maine, John Case first worked as a part-time kitchen apprentice and restaurant manager at the Mountainside Inn in Point Pleasant, Pennsylvania, where he eventually became head chef. He has also been chef at Le Bistro in Stockton, New Jersey, and is currently chef and club manager at the Rydal Country Club in Huntingdon Valley, Pennsylvania.

DENNIS GILBERT

After graduate school, Dennis Gilbert decided to combine two careers: cooking and writing. He apprenticed with a chef in Maine and trained in restaurants specializing in classical and regional French cooking. He is now *chef de cuisine* at the Vinyard Restaurant in Portland, Maine, and teaches English at the University of Southern Maine. His short stories have appeared in numerous publications.

WILLIAM RICE AND JILL VAN CLEAVE

Jill Van Cleave and her husband William Rice live, work, and cook in New York City. Currently, she is the test-kitchen supervisor at the Ketchum Food Center, a public relations firm specializing in food accounts. William Rice trained at Le Cordon Bleu in Paris and later directed a cooking school in Maryland under the auspices of Les Amis du Vin. He has been decorated by the French government for his gastronomic work and is currently editor-in-chief of *Food & Wine* magazine.

ROBERT VAN NOOD AND TIMOTHY CASS

Robert Van Nood, who was born in Holland and raised in California, apprenticed in restaurants here and abroad. Timothy Cass was formerly chef at Le Camembert and *sous chef* at Auberge Du Soleil, both in northern California, his home state. They have cooked together for many years and until recently operated the Epanoui Restaurant in Tiburon, California.

KAREN HUBERT AND LEN ALLISON

Karen Hubert and Len Allison are the chef-owners of Huberts in New York City. Their restaurant specializes in the "new American cuisine," a style of cooking characterized by the use of fresh ingredients simply prepared and elegantly presented.

French Regional Menus in Minutes
GREAT MEALS FOR FOUR IN AN HOUR OR LESS

As the twentieth-century "Prince of Gastronomes," Maurice-Edmond Sailland, better known as Curnonsky, wrote decades ago, "France is the Gastronomic Paradise of the Universe." Indeed, French contributions to gastronomy are remarkable: a profound respect for superior ingredients; an extensive, codified repertoire of recipes; and a wealth of culinary knowledge perpetuated by chefs exhaustively trained in the art of cooking. French chefs are such perfectionists that several are reputed to have committed suicide because, in their opinion, they could not live up to their reputations. In short, the French take their food seriously.

Many people associate French cuisine with elaborate sauces, subtle seasonings, expensive ingredients, and complicated kitchen procedures—the hallmarks of classic *haute cuisine*. However, it is regional dishes, originating in restaurants and homes far from the kitchens of Paris, that are the heart and soul of French cooking.

Classically trained chefs strive to create impeccable meals, blending the flavors, textures, and colors of food so precisely that both the eye *and* the palate are dazzled. After centuries of such painstaking cookery (which has its roots in the court life of the sixteenth and seventeenth centuries), a large number of recipes have become standardized. A master chef can accurately duplicate, for example, *suprêmes de volaille princesse* (boned chicken breasts served on croutons with a thick velouté sauce and garnished with truffles) or *filet de boeuf matignon* (beef tenderloin larded with salt beef tongue and thin strips of truffles, braised in Madeira, and garnished with stuffed artichoke hearts) just by hearing the dish's name. More recently, the popular *nouvelle cuisine*, or new cookery, an outgrowth of classic French cuisine, has come to emphasize the inventive use of fresh ingredients, lighter sauces, less elaborate methods of preparation, and unique presentation.

French regional cooking utilizes a wide range of ingredients, including vinegars, wines, herbs, mustards, fresh vegetables, shellfish, and poultry, opposite. Arrayed on antique French ceramic tiles (clockwise, from top right): a basket of produce; a plump duck; shallots; French cheeses, including a log of chèvre with a pepper coating; chunks of crusty fresh bread; bacon and country sausages; and a tray overflowing with produce and mussels. In the background are three pieces of French cookware.

Regional cooking, unlike *haute cuisine*, requires no highly technical cooking skills or rigid recipes; rather it is improvisational, relying on the indigenous foods—seasonal herbs and vegetables, eggs and cheeses, poultry, meats, and fresh fish—that give each region's cuisine its character. In provincial France, cooks often create recipes to suit their own tastes and the foods at hand, perhaps adding more fresh thyme to a stew or ladling fresh cream over a warm pastry. Although they do take their cooking as seriously as the country's most sophisticated chefs, French regional cooks avoid complexity and pretension—theirs is the people's cuisine.

Despite wars, food shortages, economic deprivation, and heavy influxes of foreign tourists, the traditions and recipes of French regional kitchens have persisted. Anxious to preserve their country's culinary heritage, French gastronomes began to collect regional recipes during the 1920s and 1930s, when Curnonsky published an extensive series on regional eating and drinking. *Recipes of the Provinces of France*, culled from that series, was published in the 1950s and is still widely used.

Today, regional cooking is fashionable. The French often travel hundreds of miles to sample a touted regional dish; country inns attract tourists by offering regional specialties; and provincial dishes often appear on the menus of Parisian restaurants that once considered such food beneath them.

On the following pages, nine of America's most talented cooks present 27 complete menus featuring meals from France's gastronomic regions. Each menu can be prepared in an hour or less, and all have been adapted to American ingredients and kitchens; yet each recipe retains the spirit of regional French fare, using fresh produce and good cuts of meat. Additional ingredients (vinegars, spices, herbs, and so on) are all high quality yet widely available in supermarkets or, occasionally, in specialty food shops. Each of the menus serves four people.

The cooks and the test kitchen staff have planned the meals for appearance as well as taste, as the accompanying photographs show: The vegetables are brilliant and fresh, the visual combinations appetizing. The table settings feature bright colors, simple flower arrangements, and attractive, but not necessarily expensive, serving dishes.

For each menu, the Editors, with advice from the cooks, suggest wines and other beverages. And there are suggestions for the use of leftovers and for complementary desserts. On each menu page, too, you will find a range of other tips, from a novel way to stuff chicken breasts to advice for selecting the freshest produce. All recipes have been tested meticulously to ensure that even a relatively inexperienced cook can complete a menu within an hour.

BEFORE YOU START
Great Meals in Minutes is designed for efficiency and ease. This book will work best for you if you follow these suggestions:

1. Refresh your memory with the few simple cooking techniques on the following pages. They will quickly become second nature and will help you to produce professional-quality meals in minutes.

2. Read the menus before you shop. Each lists the ingredients you will need, in the order that you would expect to shop for them in a supermarket. Many items will already be on your pantry shelf.

3. Check the equipment list on page 14. Good, sharp knives and pots and pans of the right shape and material are essential for making great meals in minutes. This may be the time to buy a few things. The right equipment can turn cooking from a necessity into a creative experience.

4. Set out everything you need before you start to cook: The lists at the beginning of each menu tell just what is required. To save effort, always keep your ingredients in the same place so you can reach for them instinctively.

5. Remove your meat, fish, and dairy products from the refrigerator early enough for them to reach room temperature.

6. Follow the start-to-finish steps for each menu. That way, you can be sure of having the entire meal ready to serve in an hour.

A NOTE ON THE FRENCH REGIONS
Since the Revolution, the legal boundaries of France's provinces have been nonexistent. However, political, geographic, and cultural boundaries remain. The regions thus created have their own character, their own customs, sometimes their own languages—and their own ways of cooking. To this day, regional names connote a particular style of cooking, based on a particular larder.

A French gastronome once observed that a dedicated eater could live to be 80 years old and not sample every regional dish, even eating a different one every day. There are, in fact, thousands of regional dishes, characteristic of particular areas, or even cities. To a large extent, nature determines the local menus. For example, where the climate is harsh, as in the Auvergne in the central plateau, farmers cultivate cabbages and sturdy root crops like potatoes. The ethnic backgrounds of regional inhabitants also contribute to their diet. In Alsace-Lorraine, people tend to eat pork and goose, noodles, and dumplings as do their German neighbors.

A GASTRONOMIC TOUR OF REGIONAL FRANCE
The following brief tour moves clockwise around France, beginning in the north, and highlights the regions and cities that have inspired the recipes in this volume.

North
In the flatlands of northern France, Champagne has played an important role in France's history, most notably as the home of Joan of Arc. Agriculturally, the region's major crops are wheat, rye, potatoes, beets, sugar beets, and grapes, and its pastures support sheep. The area's vineyards have made a major gastronomic contribution: Champagne, the universally renowned sparkling wine.

The cooks of Champagne have an excellent larder: strong cheeses, sausages, freshwater fish, dark ales, and wild game from the forests. Champagne and mushrooms characterize many local dishes. For a taste of this region's fare, Tim Cass and Robert Van Nood (page 89) offer freshwater trout in a Champagne-tarragon sauce.

Northeast
The verdant mountainous area of Alsace, in France's northeast corner, is influenced by its German neighbors across the border. Alsatians are Germanic in custom, dress, and dialect, and their cooking utilizes geese, beer, cabbage (hence the local specialty *choucroute*, or sauerkraut), Brussels sprouts, and root vegetables. Alsatians eat copious amounts of pork, whether roasted, salted, or smoked for ham and bacon, or as sausages, which are often cooked in goose or pork fat. Their *pâté de foie gras* (a paste made from the livers of specially fattened geese) rivals the famous pâté of Périgord. With possibly the richest soil in France, Alsace is noted for its grains, orchards, and vineyards. Wild game such as hare, pheasant, deer, and woodcock thrive here. Leslee Reis (pages 38–39) offers an Alsatian-style meal with a first-course sauerkraut salad followed by chicken and sausages in a white wine sauce.

East
In Burgundy, considered by many food experts to be the true seat of French gastronomy, the medieval nobility staged lavish and enormous feasts. Settled by the Baltic Burgundii in the fifth century, Burgundy comprises two distinct topographic areas: the lowlands of the Saône-Rhône and Loire rivers, and the Alps and Jura mountain ranges. The Burgundians' rich supply of ingredients includes poultry from Bresse, cattle from Charolais, root vegetables, cream, cheese, snails, black currants and cherries, morels, wild game, and freshwater perch, pike, carp, and trout.

The robust cuisine of Burgundy uses a liberal amount of garlic, Dijon mustard, purified lard, thick cream, and the region's famous wines. Foods prepared in the Burgundy style generally are cooked in a red wine sauce with mushrooms and onions, and often are garnished with lardoons (finely diced bacon). Because wine is so abundant, the best table-quality wines are freely used in cooking. William Rice and Jill Van Cleave (pages 76–77) have re-created several Burgundian-style dishes, including snails in wine sauce and pork chops with Dijon mustard.

For centuries, merchants and travelers have congregated in the city of Lyons, where today, as in the past, its inns are noted for their fine meals prepared by well-trained cooks. Although Lyons is now the third largest city in France and its surrounding area is largely industrialized, the local markets still offer a bountiful selection of potatoes, onions, salad greens, goats' and cows' milk cheeses, fruits, beef, poultry and game, and freshwater fish. Pork, particularly sausage, forms the basis of the region's hearty cuisine. Chicken or fish prepared in the Lyonnaise manner often contain a dash of vinegar, and onions are a major ingredient in several local specialities. For a taste of this cuisine, try John Case's shredded potato pie (page 61).

Southeast

Blessed with a hot, sunny climate, Provence is sometimes called the "market garden of France." As in other areas bordering the Mediterranean, the cooks of Provence have developed a cuisine based on olive oil, olives, garlic, tomatoes, saffron, sweet and hot peppers, and wild herbs. Lavender, rosemary, sage, thyme, savory, and basil grow profusely here and perfume the air.

Provençal cooking is simple and seasonal, utilizing fresh vegetables, including artichokes and eggplants, and fruit such as melons, figs, peaches, apricots, quinces, and cherries. For fish lovers, Provence is paradise, with hundreds of species indigenous to its waters. Fish stews, such as the famous Provençal *bouillabaisse*, are popular. Jacques Mokrani offers a typically Provençal shrimp main dish (pages 48–49), which contains both garlic and tomatoes.

South

The Basque country, encompassing both the coastal and mountainous areas of the Pyrénées, is home to one of the world's oldest surviving ethnic groups, the Basques. These spirited people, primarily fishermen and shepherds, rarely mingle with their French neighbors and have thus produced a unique cuisine, hardly influenced by other French cooking. In fact, Basque cooks prepare meals much the same way their ancestors did centuries ago. Their specialties include seafood and freshwater fish, Bayonne ham, mutton and goat dishes, and they flavor their dishes with onions, tomatoes, and red peppers. Jacques Mokrani's Menu 3 (pages 53–55), which features sautéed chicken, is a Basque-style meal.

Gascony is a strip of land lying between the Garonne River valley to the north and the Pyrénées to the south. This ancient province was home to D'Artagnan, one of the three swashbuckling musketeers created by Alexandre Dumas. Gascony boasts rolling hills and pine forests that shelter small game; lagoons and streams teeming with fish; and soil that produces grapes, potatoes, cabbage, and corn. Gourmets praise Gascony's fine cuisine—its goose, duck, chicken, and game bird dishes—as well as its Armagnac, the local vintage brandy. William Rice and Jill Van Cleave (pages 82–83) present a Gascony-style main course—broiled duck breast served with an Armagnac and prune sauce.

Southwest

The second largest city in France, Bordeaux is located on the Garonne River about 55 miles inland from the Bay of Biscay. Considered a major center of good eating by epicures, Bordeaux and its surrounding area epitomize regional cooking. With the sea, numerous rivers, forested mountains, and grassy plains all at hand, a Bordeaux cook is never without fresh fish, game, and produce. Various cooking styles coexist—and often overlap—in Bordeaux, providing dishes that use olive oil and garlic as well as butter and shallots. Local specialties generally call for the renowned Bordeaux wines as a cooking liquid. Jeanne Voltz (pages 31–32) features an entrée of game hens cooked in red Bordeaux wine.

The hilly Périgord region is primarily agricultural. Its lands yield an abundance of grains, vegetables, fruits and nuts, and support cattle, pigs, chickens, and the plump Toulouse geese. Périgord is renowned for two local commodities that have substantially enhanced cooking in the rest of France: *foie gras*, from the Toulouse geese, and black truffles. Truffles are walnut-sized fungi that grow on the underground roots of certain oaks. They have a delicate anise flavor and a curious fresh aroma that make them one of France's most sought-after ingredients.

The cooking of Périgord incorporates superb poultry, mushrooms, goat cheese, game, and fresh fish. Dishes cooked in the Périgord style contain truffles and often *foie gras* as well. Dennis Gilbert (page 66) offers his version of a *tourte à la périgourdine* (chicken-filled pie).

Northwest

The craggy coastline of the Brittany peninsula juts into the Bay of Biscay on its south side and the English Channel on its north. Brittany was named by the British Celts who settled there in the fifth century A.D. The Bretons have retained their ancient traditions and language (related to both Welsh and Cornish) and, like the Basques, have largely remained isolated from the rest of France. Coastal Bretons are fishermen, while those who live in the rugged interior cultivate potatoes, apples, cabbages, onions, carrots, garlic, beans, and buckwheat, and raise poultry, pigs, and *pré-salé* (salt-marsh) sheep. The cooks of Brittany, who produce a simple, hearty cuisine, are credited with the invention of the crêpe. Carol Brendlinger and Michael Wild (pages 23–25) serve earthy buckwheat crêpes as a first course and lamb chops with green beans as an entrée—both reminiscent of Brittany.

Normandy, with its coastline running along the English Channel from Brittany in the south to Picardy in the north, is flat, lushly fertile country. The region's beauty comes from its green meadows, flowering apple trees, and sparkling rivers. Its verdant farmlands are dotted with picturesque thatch-roofed farmhouses. Vikings settled here in the ninth century and their Norman descendants crossed the Channel in 1066 to conquer Britain.

The robust Normans are excellent farmers. Their prize cattle produce milk rich with nutty-sweet cream the color of ivory. Not surprisingly, both milk and cream are fundamental to Norman cooking and are the basis for one of Normandy's most famous products—cheese, in particular, Camembert. Besides cattle, Normans raise pigs,

9

Cooking at high temperatures can be dangerous, but not if you follow a few simple steps:

▶ Water added to hot fat will always cause spattering. If possible, pat foods dry with a cloth or paper towel before you add them to the hot oil in a skillet, Dutch oven, or wok.

▶ Lay the food in the pan gently, or the fat will certainly spatter.

▶ Be aware of your cooking environment. If you are boiling or steaming some foods while sautéing others, place the pots far enough apart so the water is unlikely to splash into the oil.

▶ Turn pot handles inward, toward the middle of the stove, so that you do not accidentally knock something over.

▶ Remember that alcohol—wine, brandy, or spirits—may occasionally catch fire when you add it to a very hot pan. If this happens, stand back for your own protection, and then quickly cover the pan with a lid. The fire will instantly subside, and the food will be just as good as ever.

▶ Keep pot holders and mitts close enough to be handy, but never hang them above the burners and do not lay them on the stove top.

sheep that feed on salt-marsh grass, and ducks. Coastal Normandy is famous for its seafood, particularly the true, or Dover, sole. Fertile Norman soil produces artichokes, leeks, cauliflower, and many varieties of lettuce. Although Normandy has no vineyards, its bountiful apple orchards provide cider and Calvados, an apple brandy. Most Norman cooking uses hard cider, Calvados, apples, heavy cream and butter in one form or another, and meals often end with a cream-drenched dessert. Tim Cass and Robert Van Nood offer a Norman-style meal with their chicken breasts in cream sauce (pages 86–87).

Central

The Auvergne, located on the once-volcanic central plateau of France, suffers from long winters. To stave off the cold, the peasants here have developed a hearty and highly caloric cuisine. Cabbage soup and the potato and cheese casserole called *aligot* are two of the Auvergne's notable dishes. Cooks avail themselves of local grains, cherries, peaches, apricots, nuts, salted hams, and dried sausages, and the many varieties of cheese, including Cantal. Dennis Gilbert offers two menus with recipes that illustrate Auvergnac cooking: sautéed boneless chicken breasts with parsnips accompanied by *aligot* (pages 69–70) and veal with saffron and apples (pages 72–73).

COOKING TECHNIQUES
Sautéing

Sautéing is a form of quick frying, with no cover on the pan. In French, *sauter* means "to jump," which is what vegetables or small pieces of food do when you shake the sauté pan. The purpose is to lightly brown the food and seal in the juices, sometimes before further cooking. This technique has three critical elements: the right pan, the proper temperature, and dry food.

The sauté pan: A proper sauté pan is 10 to 12 inches in diameter and has 2- to 3-inch straight sides that allow you to turn food pieces and still keep the fat from spattering. It has a heavy bottom that slides easily over a burner.

The best material (and the most expensive) for a sauté pan is tin-lined copper because it is a superior heat conductor. Heavy-gauge aluminum works well, but will discolor acidic food like tomatoes. Therefore, you should not use

aluminum if the food is to be cooked for more than twenty minutes after the initial browning. Another option is to select a heavy-duty sauté pan made of strong, heat-conducting aluminum alloys. This type of professional cookware is smooth and stick-resistant.

Use a sauté pan large enough to hold the pieces of food without crowding, or sauté in two batches. The heat of the fat and the air spaces around and between the pieces facilitate browning. Crowding results in steaming—a technique that releases juices.

Many recipes call for sautéing first, then lowering the heat and cooking the food, covered, for an additional 10 to 20 minutes. Be sure you buy a sauté pan with a tight-fitting cover. Make certain the handle is long and is comfortable to hold. Use a wooden spatula or tongs to keep food pieces moving in the pan as you shake it over the burner. If the food sticks, as it occasionally will, a metal spatula will loosen it best. Turn the pieces so that all surfaces come into contact with hot fat. Do not use a fork when sautéing meat; piercing the meat will toughen it.

Never immerse the hot pan in cold water because this will warp the metal. Allow the pan to cool slightly, then add water and let it sit until you are ready to wash it.

The fat: Half butter and half vegetable or peanut oil is perfect for most sautéing: it heats to high temperatures without burning, yet allows a rich butter flavor. For cooking, unsalted butter tastes best and adds no extra salt.

If you prefer an all-butter flavor, clarify the butter before you begin. This means removing the milky residue, which is the part that scorches. To clarify butter, heat it in a small saucepan over medium heat and, using a cooking spoon, skim off the foam as it rises to the top and discard it. Keep skimming until no more foam appears. Pour off the remaining oil, or clarified butter, leaving the milky residue at the bottom of the pan. Ideally, you should clarify only the amount of butter required by the meal you are preparing. But you can make a large quantity of it and store it in your refrigerator for two to three weeks, if desired.

Some sautéing recipes in this book call for olive oil, which imparts a delicious and distinctive flavor of its own and is less sensitive than butter to high heat.

Nevertheless, even the finest olive oil has some residue of fruit pulp, which will scorch over high heat. Watch carefully when you sauté in olive oil; discard any scorched oil and start with fresh, if necessary.

When using butter and oil together, add the butter to the hot oil. After the foam from the melting butter subsides, you are ready to sauté. If the temperature is just right, the food will sizzle when you put it in. To sauté properly, heat the fat until it is hot but not smoking. When you see small bubbles on top of the fat, it is almost hot enough to smoke. In that case, lower the heat.

Deglazing
Deglazing is an easy way to create a sauce for sautéed, braised, or roasted food. To deglaze, pour off all but 1 or 2 tablespoons of fat from the pan in which the food has been cooked. Add liquid—water, wine, or stock—and reduce the sauce over medium heat, using a wooden spoon to scrape up and blend into the sauce the concentrated juices and browned bits of food clinging to the bottom of the pan. Dennis Gilbert deglazes the skillet with white wine after sautéing veal scallops (page 73).

Poaching
You poach meat, fish, or chicken, even fruit, exactly as you would an egg, in very hot liquid in a shallow pan on top of the stove. You can use water, or better still, beef, chicken, or fish stock, or a combination of stock and white wine, or even cream. Bring the liquid to the simmering point and add the food. Lower the heat if the liquid begins to boil. Boiling toughens the food.

Blanching
Blanching, also called parboiling, is an invaluable technique. Immerse whole or cut vegetables for a few moments in boiling water, then "refresh" them, that is, plunge them into cold water to stop their cooking and set their colors. Blanching softens or tenderizes dense or crisp vegetables, often as a preliminary to further cooking by another method, such as stir frying. Jacques Mokrani blanches green beans (page 49).

Braising
Braising is long, slow simmering in a relatively small amount of liquid. Sometimes the food is browned or parboiled before braising. You may wish to flavor the braising liquid with herbs, spices, and aromatic vegetables, or use wine, stock, or tomato sauce as a medium. Leslee Reis uses this method to prepare artichoke hearts (page 44).

Broiling and Grilling
These are two relatively fast ways to cook meat, poultry, and fish, giving the food a crisp exterior while leaving the inside juicy. Whether broiling or grilling, brush the food with melted fat, a sauce, or a marinade before you cook. This adds flavor and moisture.

In broiling, the food cooks directly under the heat source. In grilling, the food cooks either directly over an open fire or on a well-seasoned cast-iron or stoneware griddle placed directly over a burner.

Roasting and Baking
Roasting is a dry-heat process, usually used for large cuts of meat and poultry, that cooks the food by exposing it to heated air in an oven or, perhaps, a covered barbecue. For more even circulation of heat, the food should be placed in a shallow pan or on a rack in a pan. For greater moisture retention, baste the food with its own juices, fat, or a flavorful marinade.

Baking applies to the dry-heat cooking of foods such as casseroles; small cuts of meat, fish, poultry, and vegetables; and, of course, breads and pastries. Some foods are baked tightly covered to retain their juices and flavors; others, such as breads, cakes, and cookies, are baked in open pans to release moisture.

Glazing
Glazing vegetables in their cooking liquid, butter, and a little sugar gives them a slight sheen as the butter and sugar reduce to a syrupy consistency. Glazing enhances the vegetables' flavor and appearance, and they need no additional sauce. William Rice and Jill Van Cleave glaze carrots (page 77).

Making Stock

Although canned chicken broth or stock is all right for emergencies, homemade chicken stock has a rich flavor that is hard to match. Moreover, the commercial broths—particularly the canned ones—are likely to be oversalted.

To make your own stock, save chicken parts as they accumulate and put them in a bag in the freezer; then have a rainy-day stock-making session, using the recipe below. The skin from a yellow onion will add color; the optional veal bone will add extra flavor and richness to the stock.

Basic Chicken Stock

3 pounds bony chicken parts, such as wings, back, and neck
1 veal knuckle (optional)
3 quarts cold water
1 yellow unpeeled onion, stuck with 2 cloves
2 stalks celery with leaves, cut in two
12 crushed peppercorns
2 carrots, scraped and cut into 2-inch lengths
4 sprigs parsley
1 bay leaf
1 tablespoon fresh thyme, or 1 teaspoon dried
Salt (optional)

1. Wash chicken parts and veal knuckle (if you are using it) and drain. Place in large soup kettle or stockpot (any big pot) with the remaining ingredients—except salt. Cover pot and bring to a boil over medium heat.

2. Lower heat and simmer stock, partly covered, 2 to 3 hours. Skim foam and scum from top of stock several times. Add salt to taste after stock has cooked 1 hour.

3. Strain stock through fine sieve placed over large bowl. Discard solids. Let stock cool uncovered (this will speed cooling process). When completely cool, refrigerate. Fat will rise and congeal conveniently at top. You may skim it off and discard it or leave it as a protective covering.

Pantry (for this volume)

A well-stocked, properly organized pantry is essential for preparing great meals in the shortest time possible. Whether your pantry consists of a small refrigerator and two or three shelves over the sink, or a large freezer, refrigerator, and entire room just off the kitchen, you must protect staples from heat and light.

In maintaining your pantry, follow these rules:

1. Store staples by kind and date. Canned goods, canisters, and spices need a separate shelf, or a separate spot on a shelf. Date all staples—shelved, refrigerated, or frozen—by writing the date directly on the package or on a bit of masking tape. Then put the oldest ones in front to be sure you use them first.

2. Store flour, sugar, and other dry ingredients in canisters or jars with tight lids. Glass and clear plastic allow you to see at a glance how much remains.

3. Keep a running grocery list so that you can note when a staple is half gone, and be sure to stock up.

ON THE SHELF:

Capers
Capers are usually packed in vinegar and less frequently in salt. If you use the latter, you should rinse them under cold water before using them.

Cornstarch
Less likely to lump than flour, cornstarch is an excellent thickener for sauces. Substitute in the following proportions: 1 tablespoon cornstarch to 2 of flour.

Flour
all-purpose, bleached or unbleached

cornmeal
May be yellow or white and of various degrees of coarseness. The stone-ground variety, milled to retain the germ of the corn, generally has a superior flavor.

Garlic
Store in a cool, dry, well-ventilated place. Garlic powder and garlic salt are not adequate substitutes for fresh garlic.

Herbs and spices
The flavor of fresh herbs is much better than that of dried. Fresh herbs should be refrigerated and used as soon as possible. The following herbs are perfectly acceptable dried, but buy in small amounts, store airtight in dry area away from heat and light, and use as quickly as possible. In measuring herbs, remember that one part dried will equal three parts fresh.

Note: Dried chives and parsley should not be on your shelf, since they have little or no flavor; frozen chives are acceptable. Buy whole spices rather than ground, as they keep their flavor much longer. Grind spices at home and store as directed for herbs.

allspice
basil
bay leaves
Cayenne pepper
cloves, whole and ground
coriander (ground)
dill
fennel seeds
marjoram
mustard (powdered)
nutmeg, whole and ground
paprika
pepper
black peppercorns
These are unripe peppercorns dried in their husks. Grind with a pepper mill for each use.
white peppercorns
These are the same as the black variety, but are picked ripe and husked. Use them in pale sauces when black pepper specks would spoil the appearance.
red pepper flakes (also called crushed red pepper)
rosemary
saffron
Made from the dried stigmas of a species of crocus, this spice—the most costly of all seasonings—adds both color and flavor. Use sparingly.

salt
Use coarse salt—commonly available as Kosher or sea—for its superior flavor, texture, and purity. Kosher salt and sea salt are less salty than table salt. Substitute in the following proportions: three-quarters teaspoon table salt equals just under one teaspoon Kosher or sea salt.

tarragon
thyme

Hot pepper sauce

Nuts, whole, chopped or slivered
pine nuts (pignoli)
walnuts

Oils
corn, safflower, or vegetable
Because these neutral-tasting oils have high smoking points, they are good for high-heat sautéing.

olive oil
Sample French, Greek, Spanish, and Italian oils. Olive oil ranges in color from pale yellow to dark green and in taste from mild and delicate to rich and fruity. Different olive oils can be used for different purposes: for example, lighter ones for cooking, stronger ones for salads. The finest quality olive oil is labeled extra-virgin or virgin.

walnut oil
Rich and nutty tasting. It turns rancid easily, so keep it in a tightly closed container in the refrigerator.

Onions
Store all dry-skinned onions in a cool, dry, well-ventilated place.

red or Italian onions
Zesty tasting and generally eaten raw. The perfect salad onion.

shallots
The most subtle member of the onion family, the shallot has a delicate garlic flavor.

yellow onions
All-purpose cooking onions, strong in taste.

Potatoes, boiling and baking
"New" potatoes are not a particular kind of potato, but any potato that has not been stored.

Rice
long-grain white rice
Slender grains, much longer than they are wide, that become light and fluffy when cooked and are best for general use.

Stock, chicken and beef
For maximum flavor and quality, your own stock is best (see recipe page 11), but canned stock, or broth, is adequate for most recipes and convenient to have on hand.

Sugar
light brown sugar
granulated sugar

Tomatoes
Italian plum tomatoes
Canned plum tomatoes (preferably imported) are an acceptable substitute for fresh.

Vanilla extract

Vinegars

apple cider vinegar (also called cider vinegar)
> Use for a mild, fruity flavor.

balsamic vinegar
> Aged vinegar with a complex sweet and sour taste

red and white wine vinegars

raspberry vinegar
> Made by steeping fresh berries and sugar in vinegar.

tarragon vinegar
> A white wine vinegar flavored with fresh tarragon, it is especially good in salads.

Wines and spirits

Cognac or brandy
sherry, sweet and dry
red wine, dry
vermouth, dry
white wine, dry
Worcestershire sauce

IN THE REFRIGERATOR:

Basil
> Though fresh basil is widely available only in summer, try to use it whenever possible to replace dried; the flavor is markedly superior. Stand the stems, preferably with roots intact, in a jar of water, and loosely cover leaves with a plastic bag.

Bread crumbs
> You need never buy bread crumbs. To make fresh crumbs, use fresh or day-old bread and process in food processor or blender. For dried, toast bread 30 minutes in preheated 250-degree oven, turning occasionally to prevent slices from browning. Proceed as for fresh. Store bread crumbs in an airtight container: fresh crumbs in the refrigerator, and dried crumbs in a cool, dry place. Either type may also be frozen for several weeks if tightly wrapped in a plastic bag.

Butter
> Many cooks prefer unsalted butter because of its finer flavor and because it does not burn as easily as salted.

Cheese

Cheddar cheese, sharp
> A firm cheese, ranging in color from nearly white to yellow. Cheddar is a versatile cooking cheese.

goat cheese, log type
> Goat cheese, or *chèvre*, has a distinctive, tangy taste. It comes in many shapes (for example, a log), either plain or rolled in finely powdered ash. The ash gives it a slightly salty taste.

Parmesan cheese
> Avoid the preground packaged variety; it is very expensive and almost flavorless. Buy Parmesan by the quarter- or half-pound wedge and grate as needed: 4 ounces produces about one cup of grated cheese. Romano, far less costly, can be substituted, but its flavor is considerably sharper—or try mixing the two.

Chives
> Refrigerate fresh chives wrapped in plastic. You may also buy small pots of growing chives—keep them on a windowsill and snip as needed.

Cream
half-and-half
heavy cream

Eggs
> Will keep 4 to 5 weeks in refrigerator. For best results, bring to room temperature before using.

Ginger, fresh
> Found in the produce section. Ginger will stay fresh in the refrigerator for approximately 1 week, wrapped in plastic. To preserve it longer, place the whole ginger root in a small sherry-filled jar; it will last almost indefinitely, although not without changes in the ginger. Or, if you prefer, store it in the freezer, where it will last about 3 months. Newly purchased ginger need not be peeled.

Lemons
> In addition to its many uses in cooking, a slice of lemon rubbed over cut apples and pears will keep them from discoloring. Do not substitute bottled juice or lemon extract.

Limes
Milk
Mint
> Fresh mint will keep for a week if wrapped in a damp paper towel and enclosed in a plastic bag.

Mustards
> The recipes in this book usually call for Dijon or coarse-ground mustard.

Parsley
> The two most commonly available kinds of parsley are flat-leaved and curly; they can be used interchangeably when necessary. Flat-leaved parsley has a more distinctive flavor and is generally preferred in cooking. Curly parsley wilts less easily and is excellent for garnishing. Store parsley in a glass of water and cover loosely with a plastic bag. It will keep for a week in the refrigerator. Or wash and dry it, and refrigerate in a small plastic bag with a dry paper towel inside to absorb any moisture.

Scallions
> Scallions have a mild onion flavor. Store wrapped in plastic.

Equipment

Proper cooking equipment makes the work light and is a good cook's most prized possession. You can cook expertly without a store-bought steamer or even a food processor, but basic pans, knives, and a few other items are indispensable. Below are the things you need—and some attractive options—for preparing the menus in this volume.

Pots and pans
Large kettle or stockpot
3 skillets (large, medium, small), with covers
2 heavy-gauge sauté pans, 10 to 12 inches in diameter, with covers and ovenproof handles
3 saucepans with covers (1-, 2-, and 4-quart capacities)
  Choose heavy-gauge enameled cast-iron, plain cast-iron, aluminum-clad stainless steel, and aluminum (but you need at least one saucepan that is not aluminum). Best—but very expensive—is tin-lined copper.
8-inch omelet pan
Roasting pan
Broiler pan
2 shallow baking pans (13 x 9 x 2-inch and 8 x 8-inch)
2 cookie sheets (11 x 17-inch and 15 x 10-inch)
Medium-size soufflé dish
Flameproof casserole with tight-fitting cover
Large flameproof glass baking dish
Heatproof serving bowl
Heatproof serving platter
Four 4-ounce ramekins or *pots de crème*
9-inch pie plate
9-inch tart pan
Salad bowl

Knives
A carbon-steel knife takes a sharp edge but tends to rust. You must wash and dry it after each use; otherwise it can blacken foods and counter tops. Good-quality stainless steel knives, frequently honed, are less trouble and will serve just as well in the home kitchen. Never put a fine knife in the dishwasher. Rinse it, dry it, and put it away—but not loose in a drawer. Knives will stay sharp and last a long time if they have their own storage rack.
Small paring knife
10-inch chef's knife
Sharpening steel

Other cooking tools
2 sets of mixing bowls in graduated sizes
Colander, with a round base (stainless steel, aluminum, or enamel)
2 strainers in fine and coarse mesh
2 sets of measuring cups and spoons in graduated sizes
  One for dry ingredients, another for shortenings and liquids.
Small jar with tight-fitting lid
Cooking spoon
Slotted spoon
Long-handled wooden spoons
Wooden spatula (for stirring hot ingredients)
2 metal spatulas, or turners (for lifting hot foods from pans)
Slotted spatula
Rubber or vinyl spatula (for folding in ingredients)
Rolling pin
Grater (metal, with several sizes of holes)
  A rotary grater is handy for hard cheese.
2 wire whisks
Pair of metal tongs
Wooden board
Potato masher
Garlic press
Vegetable peeler
Mortar and pestle
Vegetable steamer
Ladle
Pastry brush for basting (a small, new paintbrush that is not nylon serves well)
Large wooden toothpicks or small skewers
Cooling rack
Kitchen shears
Kitchen timer
Aluminum foil
Paper towels
Plastic wrap
Waxed paper
Thin rubber gloves

Electric appliances
Food processor or blender
  A blender will do most of the work required in this volume, but a food processor will do it more quickly and in larger volume. A food processor should be considered a necessity, not a luxury, for anyone who enjoys cooking.
Electric mixer

Optional cooking tools
Cast-iron griddle
Salad spinner
Meat grinder
Mandoline
Apple corer
Salad servers
Citrus juicer
  Inexpensive glass kind from the dime store will do.
Nutmeg grater
Melon baller
Kitchen mallet
Flametamer or asbestos mat
Bulb baster
Zester
Pastry cutter
Roll of masking tape or white paper tape for labeling and dating

GRATER

COLANDER

STRAINER

FOOD PROCESSOR

RUBBER SPATULA

SLOTTED SPATULA

METAL SPATULA

MIXING BOWLS

WHISK

PARING KNIFE

CHEF'S KNIFE

SHARPENING STEEL

DOUBLE BOILER

CASSEROLE

SAUCEPANS

SAUTÉ PAN

ON   PULSE / OFF

Carol Brendlinger and Michael Wild

As a girl, Carol Brendlinger cooked for her six younger siblings, but she never thought about being a chef until she got her first job—cooking three meals a day for 110 people at a camp in the middle of the Arizona desert. After this rugged yet enjoyable apprenticeship, she returned to San Francisco and worked her way up from salad chef to head chef in local restaurants.

For Michael Wild, his French mother and his own extensive travels were his culinary inspiration. "My mother cooked anywhere with whatever was at hand. So, I learned to shop and cook anywhere, too," he says. Today, wherever he goes, he seeks out "real" cooking.

Though their backgrounds differ sharply, Carol Brendlinger and Michael Wild have developed compatible cooking styles. For these menus, they utilize foods commonly associated with certain regions of France and combine them with some unexpected ingredients.

Menu 1, for example, calls for a number of ingredients characteristic of Provençal cooking—garlic, olive oil, fresh herbs, anchovies, and tomatoes. The cooks add goat cheese, Greek olives, and chili peppers to come up with their unusual appetizer and swordfish entrée.

For their hearty Menu 2 dinner from Alsace, they offer such typical dishes as garlic sausages and red cabbage simmered with Alsatian Riesling, but add surprises such as hazelnuts, juniper berries, and fresh ginger to the sausage, and raspberry vinegar to the salad dressing.

Menu 3 is more traditional. Here they use buckwheat flour, scallops, apples, cider, lamb, cream, butter, and Calvados to create a meal that you might find any day in Brittany.

A fluted tart filled with goat cheese, Greek olives, red pepper, red onion, and anchovies makes an unusual first course. The entrée of swordfish steaks is served with an herb- and chili-enhanced tomato sauce and is garnished with orange sections and chopped scallions.

17

Open-Faced Goat Cheese Tart
Swordfish with Spicy Tomato-Orange Sauce

The dramatic, colorful goat cheese tart calls for several unusual ingredients. The crust contains polenta, a type of cornmeal used as a staple in Italy. For the tart's topping, select a fresh mild-flavored goat cheese, such as Montrachet. Or, if you prefer, combine feta cheese with cream cheese. Kalamata olives are juicy, slightly bitter purple-black Greek olives cured in vinegar.

Swordfish is a firm-textured oily fish. If it is unavailable, suitable substitutes are shark, tuna, goosefish, or any other firm, white fish.

WHAT TO DRINK

These Provençal flavors will match a full-bodied, dry white wine from the Rhône Valley such as a white Châteauneuf-du-Pape or Crozes-Hermitages.

SHOPPING LIST AND STAPLES

Four ½- to ¾-inch-thick swordfish steaks (about 1½ pounds total weight)
1 red bell pepper
3 medium-size ripe tomatoes (about 1¾ pounds total weight)
2 small red onions
Large bunch scallions
5 cloves garlic
2 fresh medium-hot chilies, or 1 teaspoon to 1 tablespoon red pepper flakes
Large bunch mixed herbs, such as basil, thyme, or oregano
2 oranges
1 lemon
½ pint heavy cream
½ pound goat cheese
Two 3½-ounce cans anchovy fillets
11-ounce can Kalamata olives, or 6-ounce can pitted black olives
¾ cup olive oil
1 cup flour
½ cup polenta or coarse cornmeal
Salt and freshly gound black pepper
½ cup dry white wine or dry vermouth

UTENSILS

Large skillet or sauté pan with cover
Broiler pan
9-inch tart pan
Cooling rack
Large heatproof serving platter
2 large mixing bowls
Measuring cups and spoons
Chef's knife
Paring knife
Wooden spoon
Metal spatula
Juicer
Rubber gloves (if using fresh chilies)
Basting brush

START-TO-FINISH STEPS

1. Prepare onions, garlic, scallions, and mixed herbs for tart and swordfish recipes.
2. Follow tart recipe steps 1 through 6.
3. Remove crust from oven and follow swordfish recipe steps 1 through 4.
4. While sauce is reducing, follow tart recipe steps 7 and 8.
5. While tart is baking, follow swordfish recipe step 5.
6. When tart is done, follow swordfish recipe step 6 and serve tart as first course.
7. Follow swordfish recipe steps 7 through 10 and serve.

RECIPES

Open-Faced Goat Cheese Tart

The crust:
½ cup coarse polenta or coarse cornmeal
1 cup flour
Pinch of salt
¼ cup olive oil

The topping:
½ pound goat cheese
½ cup heavy cream
¼ cup minced mixed herbs
2 cloves garlic, peeled and minced
10 to 15 Kalamata olives or pitted black olives
1 red bell pepper
½ small red onion, peeled and thinly sliced
6 scallion tops, thinly sliced
10 anchovy fillets, soaked in cold water to remove salt, if desired

1. Preheat oven to 450 degrees.

2. For crust, combine dry ingredients in large bowl. Add olive oil and stir until blended. Add ¼ cup cold water. The dough will be very firm. If crumbly, add 1 tablespoon water to make dough stick together.

3. Press dough firmly and evenly into 9-inch tart pan. Prick bottom of crust with fork.

4. Bake crust until edges are slightly browned, 10 to 15 minutes. Transfer pan to rack to cool.

5. While crust is baking, make filling: Pit olives, if using Kalamatas, and slice thinly. Wash bell pepper and pat dry. Halve, core, and seed pepper; cut half of pepper into dice.

6. In large bowl, beat goat cheese, cream, herbs, and garlic into a thick paste.

7. Spread mixture over crust. Arrange olives, bell pepper, onion, scallions, and anchovies in circles on top.

8. Bake 10 minutes, or just until heated through. Serve as soon as possible so that crust does not become soggy.

Swordfish with Spicy Tomato-Orange Sauce

3 medium-size ripe tomatoes
2 fresh medium-hot chilies, or 1 teaspoon to 1 tablespoon red pepper flakes
2 oranges
1 lemon
½ cup olive oil
Small red onion, peeled and finely chopped
3 cloves garlic, peeled and minced
2 tablespoons minced mixed herbs
½ cup dry white wine or dry vermouth
Four ½- to ¾-inch-thick swordfish steaks
Salt and freshly ground black pepper
2 to 3 chopped scallions for garnish

1. Peel, seed, and chop tomatoes. If using fresh chilies, rinse and pat dry. Split in half lengthwise and remove membranes and seeds. Cut into small dice.

2. Peel 1 orange and cut into sections. Squeeze juice from lemon and remaining orange.

3. In large skillet, heat ¼ cup olive oil over medium heat. Add onion, chilies, garlic, and herbs, and sauté, stirring with wooden spoon, until soft, about 5 minutes.

4. Add wine and fruit juices, increase heat to high, and boil briskly until reduced to a syrup, 4 to 6 minutes.

5. Add tomatoes and cook just until heated through, 1 minute. Season with salt and pepper to taste, cover, and remove pan from heat.

6. Preheat broiler. Arrange swordfish steaks on broiler pan and brush each with 1 tablespoon of remaining olive oil.

7. Broil swordfish 2 to 3 inches from heating element, about 5 minutes per side (depending on thickness), until almost opaque. Turn steaks carefully using metal spatula.

8. While fish is broiling, reheat sauce briefly, if necessary.

9. Spoon some sauce onto heatproof serving platter and arrange fish on top. Spoon more sauce over fish and garnish with orange sections and scallions.

10. Set platter under broiler to heat oranges and allow fish to finish cooking, about 2 minutes. Serve immediately.

Although this puffy, light dessert requires lengthy preparation, the results are worth the effort. Brandy-flavored crepes form the crust of the apricot-flavored soufflé, and puréed apricots that have been simmered in white wine make up the sauce. Save the extra two or three leftover crepes for a snack.

Apricot Soufflé Crêpes

The sauce:
¼ pound dried apricots
3 cups dry white wine, approximately

The crêpes:
1 cup flour, approximately
2 eggs
¾ cup half-and-half or light cream
1 tablespoon Calvados or brandy
2 tablespoons sugar
Pinch of salt
2 tablespoons unsalted butter, melted

The soufflé:
2 eggs
¼ cup sugar

1. For the sauce, combine apricots and 2 cups wine in small saucepan and bring to a boil over high heat. Lower heat and simmer 20 minutes.

2. Transfer apricots and wine to food processor or food mill and purée. Set aside.

3. For the crêpes, combine crêpe ingredients in large mixing bowl, using only enough flour to make a slightly runny batter.

4. Place a small well-seasoned or nonstick skillet over medium-high heat. Add a few tablespoons of batter, tilting and turning the skillet so batter covers bottom evenly, and cook 1 to 2 minutes, or until lightly colored. Turn crêpe and cook another 30 seconds. Turn crêpe out onto wax paper. Cover with another sheet of waxed paper. Repeat with remaining batter. There should be enough batter for 6 or 7 crêpes.

5. Butter four 4- to 5-inch tart molds. Fit 1 crêpe into each; the edges should stick out in folds.

6. For soufflé, preheat oven to 375 degrees. Separate eggs. In large bowl, beat whites with electric mixer at high speed until stiff. Add sugar and beat another minute.

7. In small bowl, mix yolks with ⅓ cup reserved apricot purée. Stir in a spoonful of whites to lighten yolk mixture. With rubber spatula, gently fold yolk mixture into whites just until incorporated.

8. Divide soufflé mixture among the 4 "molded" crêpes. Bake 15 to 20 minutes, until puffed and brown. Transfer to a rack.

9. In small saucepan, heat remaining apricot purée, adding enough wine to make a thin sauce.

10. Spoon sauce around edges of 4 plates. Tilting mold, gently nudge each soufflé out into center of plate. Drizzle with additional sauce and serve immediately.

Garlic Sausages with Red Cabbage and Juniper Berry Sauce
Cucumber, Beet, and Onion Salad

The sausages, made of ground pork, duck, and veal, are seasoned with an unusual combination of hazelnuts, juniper berries, and ginger. If desired, a natural casing for these patties can be formed with caul fat, bought in sheets from your butcher.

WHAT TO DRINK

This Alsatian meal demands a wine from its native region: an Alsatian Riesling or a Sylvaner.

The vivid colors of the salad and the main course make this a festive meal. Arrange the sausage patties, garnished with watercress, on a bed of the baked cabbage, and serve the creamy juniper berry sauce for the sausages on the side.

SHOPPING LIST AND STAPLES

2 pounds uncooked meat, unground (a mixture of pork, duck, and veal or any two combined)
½ pound caul fat (optional)
3 young beets (about ½ pound total weight)
½ head red cabbage (about 1¼ pounds)
Large cucumber, or 2 small cucumbers
Large bunch watercress
Small bunch chives
2 medium-size red onions
6 shallots
6 cloves garlic
3-inch piece fresh ginger
5 lemons

5 apples, preferably Granny Smith or Pippin
   (about 2 pounds total weight)
1 pint heavy cream
2 tablespoons olive oil
¾ cup raspberry vinegar
2 tablespoons sugar (optional)
¼ pound hazelnuts
3 tablespoons juniper berries
Salt and freshly ground black pepper
3 cups dry white wine, preferably Riesling

UTENSILS

Food processor or meat grinder
Small sauté pan
Medium-size nonaluminum saucepan
Small saucepan
Large baking dish
15 x 10-inch baking sheet
2 large bowls
Medium-size bowl
3 small bowls
Salad spinner (optional)
Measuring cups and spoons
Chef's knife
Paring knife

Wooden spoon
Rubber spatula
Grater (if not using food processor)
Juicer
Apple corer (optional)

START-TO-FINISH STEPS

1. For sausages and sauce recipes, toast juniper berries in small, dry sauté pan until firm and puffed, 3 to 4 minutes. Juice lemons for cabbage, sauce, and salad recipes.
2. Follow cabbage recipe steps 1 through 3.
3. Follow sausages recipe steps 1 through 10.
4. Follow salad recipe step 1.
5. Follow sauce recipe steps 1 and 2.
6. While sauce is reducing, follow salad recipe steps 2 through 5.
7. Follow sauce recipe steps 3 and 4.
8. Follow salad recipe steps 6 and 7, sausages recipe step 11, sauce recipe step 5, and serve.

RECIPES

Garlic Sausages with Red Cabbage

2 pounds uncooked meat, unground (a mixture of pork, duck, and veal or any two combined)

½ cup hazelnuts
½ pound caul fat (optional)
4 shallots
6 cloves garlic
1 tablespoon juniper berries, toasted
2-inch piece fresh ginger
1 teaspoon salt
2 apples, preferably Granny Smith or Pippin
   (about ¾ pound total weight)
Freshly ground black pepper
Red Cabbage (see following recipe)
Watercress sprigs for garnish (optional)

1. Preheat oven to 375 degrees.
2. In food processor fitted with metal blade or with meat grinder, grind meats until fairly smooth. Transfer to large bowl and set aside. Rinse out processor bowl.
3. Arrange hazelnuts in a single layer on baking sheet and toast in oven until light brown, about 12 minutes. Remove nuts from oven and rub with paper towels to remove skins. Set aside.
4. If using caul fat, soak in large bowl of cold water at least 10 minutes.
5. Peel shallots and garlic. In food processor or with chef's knife, mince shallots, garlic, juniper berries, and ginger with 1 teaspoon salt. Add to meat.
6. In processor or with chef's knife, coarsely chop hazelnuts and add to meat mixture.
7. If desired, peel apples; halve and core. In processor fitted with shredding disk or with grater, shred apples.
8. Add apples and pepper to taste to meat mixture, and mix well with your hands.
9. Drain caul fat and pat dry. Using about ¾ cup for each sausage, form mixture into patties and wrap in caul fat, if using.
10. Place patties on top of red cabbage mixture and bake 30 minutes, until lightly golden.
11. Divide cabbage among 4 large plates. Place 2 sausage patties on each plate and garnish with watercress sprigs, if desired.

Red Cabbage

Medium-size red onion
½ head red cabbage (about 1¼ pounds)
3 apples, preferably Granny Smith or Pippin (about
   1¼ pounds total weight)
Juice of 2 lemons (about ½ cup)
1 cup dry white wine, preferably Riesling

1. Peel onion. In food processor fitted with slicing disk or with chef's knife, thinly slice cabbage and onion, and transfer to large baking dish.
2. If desired, peel apples; halve and core. In food processor fitted with shredding disk or with grater, grate apples. Transfer apples to large bowl and toss with lemon juice and wine.
3. Turn mixture into baking dish and toss with cabbage and onion. Set aside.

Juniper Berry Sauce

1 pint heavy cream
2 tablespoons juniper berries, toasted
1-inch piece fresh ginger
2 shallots
2 cups dry white wine, preferably Riesling
Juice of 1 lemon (about ¼ cup)
Salt and freshly ground black pepper

1. In medium-size nonaluminum saucepan, combine cream, juniper berrries, and ginger, and cook slowly over low heat until cream has reduced to 1 cup, 15 to 20 minutes.
2. While cream is reducing, peel and mince shallots. In small saucepan, combine shallots, wine, and lemon juice, and cook over medium-high heat until liquid has reduced to ½ cup, about 10 minutes.
3. Lower heat to medium and stir in wine mixture.
4. Remove ginger, and season sauce with salt and pepper to taste. Remove pan from heat, cover, and keep warm.
5. Transfer sauce to sauceboat or small bowl.

Cucumber, Beet, and Onion Salad

3 young beets (about ½ pound total weight)
¾ cup raspberry vinegar
Juice of 2 lemons (about ½ cup)
2½ teaspoons salt
Freshly ground black pepper
2 tablespoons sugar (optional)
Large cucumber, or 2 small cucumbers
Medium-size red onion
Large bunch watercress
Small bunch chives
2 tablespoons olive oil

1. Peel beets. In food processor fitted with metal blade or with grater, grate beets. In small bowl, combine beets with ½ cup raspberry vinegar, 2 tablespoons lemon juice, 1 teaspoon salt, and pepper to taste. Check seasoning: If beets are not sweet, add 1 tablespoon sugar.
2. Peel cucumber, halve lengthwise, and, using teaspoon, seed, if necessary. Cut cucumber on diagonal into ⅛-inch-thick slices. In another small bowl, combine cucumber with ¼ cup lemon juice, 1½ teaspoons salt, pepper to taste, and remaining 1 tablespoon sugar.
3. Peel onion and cut into ⅛-inch-thick slices. In small bowl, combine onion with 2 cups cold water and remaining ¼ cup raspberry vinegar.
4. Wash watercress and dry in salad spinner or pat dry with paper towels. Remove tough stems and discard. Wrap watercress in paper towels and refrigerate until ready to serve.
5. Wash chives and pat dry with paper towels. Chop coarsely and set aside.
6. Just before serving, place watercress in medium-size bowl and toss with olive oil.
7. Drain vegetables and pat dry with paper towels. Arrange vegetables and watercress in concentric circles on salad plates and sprinkle with chives.

Crêpes with Scallops and Calvados Beurre Blanc
Broiled Lamb Chops with Parsley Butter
Green Beans and Carrots in Garlic-Cream Sauce

Buckwheat crêpes topped with scallops in butter sauce can precede the thick lamb chops and julienne carrots and beans.

Buckwheat crêpes, scallops, and *beurre blanc*, here united for a rich first course, are quintessential elements of Brittany's cuisine. In particular, buckwheat flour is a staple ingredient that appears in many Breton dishes. Because buckwheat flour has a strong nutlike flavor, most recipes, including this one, call for combining it with wheat flour for a milder taste. For this recipe, the buckwheat flour should not be sifted. Buy it at health food stores or specialty food shops and store it in an airtight container in a cool, dry place.

This unusual version of the classic *beurre blanc*, or white butter sauce, typically served with seafood, is an emulsion of wine, Calvados, apple juice, minced shallot, and chilled butter. The *beurre blanc* remains creamy during cooking because you add the butter slowly while stirring over low heat to keep the sauce from boiling. Too much heat causes the sauce to separate. Calvados, a dry apple brandy distilled from apple cider, is named for an area bordering the English Channel in Normandy. Aged Calvados is best for drinking, but an immature Calvados will do for cooking, giving sauces a mild apple flavor. Fine liquor stores sell Calvados, but American applejack or apple-flavored brandies, which are more widely available and less costly, are acceptable substitutes.

If you can find good, dry cider, try it with this Breton menu. A simple, crisp white wine, such as a French Muscadet or Italian Verdicchio, would taste fine with the first course. The cook suggests an older California Cabernet or Pinot Noir for the broiled lamb, but a good Saint-Émilion would serve equally well. If you're feeling truly Breton, have a small glass of Calvados after your dessert as a *digestif*.

SHOPPING LIST AND STAPLES

Four 2-inch-thick lamb chops (about 2 pounds total weight)
½ pound bay scallops
Large carrot (about ¼ pound)
1 red bell pepper
½ pound green beans
2 shallots
4 cloves garlic
1 bunch chives
1 bunch parsley
3 lemons
1 green apple
1 egg
½ pint half-and-half
1 pint heavy cream
2 sticks unsalted butter
½ cup unfiltered apple juice
¼ cup buckwheat flour
¼ cup all-purpose flour
Salt
Freshly ground black and white pepper
¼ cup plus 1 tablespoon Calvados
1 cup dry white wine

UTENSILS

Food processor (optional)
Griddle or large skillet
Large sauté pan or skillet
Broiler pan
2 small saucepans
Heatproof platter
2 small mixing bowls
Measuring cups and spoons
Chef's knife
Paring knife
Wooden spoon
Metal spatula
Juicer

START-TO-FINISH STEPS

1. Juice lemons for beurre blanc and lamb chops recipes. Follow beurre blanc recipe steps 1 and 2.
2. Follow crêpes recipe step 1.

3. Follow lamb chops recipe steps 1 and 2.
4. Follow green beans recipe steps 1 and 2.
5. Follow scallops recipe steps 1 through 3.
6. Follow crêpes recipe steps 2 and 3.
7. Follow beurre blanc recipe step 3.
8. Follow lamb chops recipe step 3, scallops recipe steps 4 through 7, and serve with crêpes for first course.
9. Follow green beans recipe step 3 and lamb chops recipe steps 4 and 5.
10. Follow green beans recipe step 4, lamb chops recipe step 6, and serve.

RECIPES

Crêpes with Scallops and Calvados Beurre Blanc

1 green apple
1 bunch chives
1 red bell pepper
2 tablespoons unsalted butter
½ pound bay scallops
Salt
Freshly ground black pepper
Crêpes (see following recipe)
Calvados Beurre Blanc (see following recipe)

1. Preheat oven to 250 degrees.
2. Halve, core, and dice apple. Wash chives and pat dry with paper towels; finely chop enough to measure 2 tablespoons. Rinse bell pepper and pat dry with paper towels. Halve, core, and seed pepper; dice enough to measure ½ cup.
3. Place 4 dinner plates in oven to warm.
4. In large sauté pan, melt butter over medium heat. Add apple and pepper, cook, stirring occasionally, 2 minutes.
5. Add scallops and cook, stirring, 2 minutes.
6. Season to taste with salt and pepper and add chives.
7. Divide crêpes equally among 4 warm plates. Spoon scallop mixture over crêpes and top each serving with beurre blanc.

Crêpes

1 tablespoon unsalted butter
¼ cup buckwheat flour
¼ cup all-purpose flour
½ cup half-and-half
1 egg
1 tablespoon Calvados
Pinch of salt

1. In small heavy-gauge saucepan or butter warmer, melt butter.
2. In small bowl, combine all ingredients, including butter.
3. Lightly butter griddle or large skillet and place over medium heat. Drop batter by tablespoonfuls to make 3-inch pancakes. Cook about 30 seconds per side, or until lightly browned. As crêpes are cooked, transfer them to

heatproof platter and keep warm in oven until ready to serve. Repeat with remaining batter; you will have about 20 crêpes.

Calvados Beurre Blanc

1 shallot
1 cup dry white wine
½ cup unfiltered apple juice
¼ cup Calvados
Juice of 2 lemons (about ½ cup)
1 stick unsalted butter, chilled
Salt
Freshly ground pepper

1. Peel and mince shallot.
2. In small saucepan, combine wine, apple juice, Calvados, lemon juice, and shallot. Simmer mixture gently over low heat until reduced to a syrupy glaze, about 30 minutes.
3. Cut butter into tablespoon-size pieces and add to glaze, 1 tablespoon at a time, stirring until each piece is incorporated before adding the next. Keep sauce on heat just until barely warm and last piece of butter has melted or sauce will separate. Add salt and pepper to taste.

Broiled Lamb Chops with Parsley Butter

1 bunch parsley
2 cloves garlic
1 shallot
1 teaspoon salt
5 tablespoons unsalted butter, at room temperature
Juice of 1 lemon (about ¼ cup)
Four 2-inch-thick lamb chops (about 2 pounds
    total weight)
½ cup heavy cream

1. Peel garlic and shallot. In food processor or with chef's knife, chop parsley, garlic, shallot, and salt.
2. In small bowl, blend parsley mixture with butter and lemon juice. Set aside.
3. Preheat broiler.
4. Trim fat off lamb chops and discard. Arrange chops in single layer on broiler pan and top each with ½ tablespoon of cream. Broil 3 to 4 inches from heating element, 6 minutes for rare, 8 minutes for medium, or 10 minutes for well done.
5. Turn chops and top each with another spoonful of cream. Continue broiling another 6 to 10 minutes.
6. Transfer chops to heatproof serving platter and top each with a spoonful of parsley butter. Place platter under broiler 1 minute to melt butter. Transfer chops to individual plates.

Green Beans and Carrots in Garlic-Cream Sauce

½ pound green beans
Large carrot (about ¼ pound)

2 cloves garlic
1 cup heavy cream
Salt
Freshly ground black pepper

1. Remove stem ends from beans. Wash beans, pat dry with paper towels, and cut into julienne.
2. Peel carrot and cut into 2-inch-long pieces. Halve each piece lengthwise and cut into julienne. Peel garlic.
3. In small saucepan, combine green beans, carrot, garlic, cream, and salt and pepper to taste, and bring to a boil over high heat. Reduce heat to low and simmer 10 minutes, or until vegetables are crisp-tender.
4. Remove and discard garlic cloves, and turn vegetables into serving bowl.

ADDED TOUCH

Madeleines are small sweet cakes baked in a madeleine mold, which has indentations shaped like elongated scallop shells. Here the madeleines are flavored with orange-flower water, a fragrant liquid made from distilled orange blossoms. Liquor stores and pharmacies usually stock orange-flower water.

Madeleines

1 stick plus 2 tablespoons unsalted butter
1 lime
1 lemon
3 eggs
⅔ cup sugar
½ teaspoon vanilla extract
1 tablespoon orange-flower water, or grated zest of
    ½ orange
1 cup plus 1 tablespoon all-purpose flour
½ teaspoon baking powder

1. In small heavy-gauge saucepan or butter warmer, melt butter over low heat. Set aside to cool.
2. Grate zest from lemon and lime, and squeeze enough lemon to measure 1 tablespoon juice.
3. In large bowl, combine eggs and sugar, and beat with electric mixer until almost stiff.
4. Add lemon and lime zest, lemon juice, vanilla extract, and orange-flower water, and beat a few more minutes, until well blended.
5. Sift together 1 cup of flour and baking powder. Using rubber spatula, gently fold into batter. Stir in 8 tablespoons of melted butter.
6. Set the batter aside to rest in a cool place at least 15 minutes or up to 2 hours.
7. Meanwhile, preheat oven to 350 degrees.
8. In small bowl, combine remaining 2 tablespoons melted butter with remaining 1 tablespoon flour. Brush madeleine molds with mixture. Add enough batter to fill each mold two thirds full.
9. Bake 10 to 15 minutes, or until madeleines are slightly browned at the edges. Transfer to a rack to cool.

Jeanne Voltz

MENU 1 (Right)
**Carrot Soup
Boeuf Bourguignon Sauté
Butter-Braised Broccoli**

MENU 2
**Chicken Liver and Lettuce Salad
Game Hens in Claret
Cauliflower au Gratin**

MENU 3
**Mushrooms with Snail Butter
Broiled Butterflied Leg of Lamb in Red Wine
Crock-Roasted Potatoes**

All her life, food writer Jeanne Voltz has been a Francophile. As a girl, she envied the American literary figures who lived in Paris—Hemingway, the Fitzgeralds, Gertrude Stein. Daily, they sampled the cuisine she could only read about in novels. When she finally visited France as an adult, she "could hardly taste fast enough or eat enough" to satisfy her curiosity and long-time envy. Nothing had prepared her for the excitement of the exquisite foods she ate.

Jeanne Voltz has made many pilgrimages to France and found it difficult to decide which of her favorite dishes to present here. Her Menu 1, a hearty family meal, features a full-flavored carrot soup, *boeuf bourguignon*, the renowned main dish from Burgundy, and butter-braised broccoli. The beef entrée is normally slow-cooked (3 to 4 hours), but this version calls for a tender cut of beef, cubed for quick sautéing.

In Menu 2, two recipes are reminiscent of Bordeaux— game hens in red wine and cauliflower au gratin. The warm chicken liver salad is a variation on a recipe from nearby Gascony, where warm *foie gras* is a prelude to many meals.

Menu 3 features broiled butterflied leg of lamb, mushrooms stuffed with snail butter (which contains no snails but is so-called because it is always used to fill *escargots à la bourguignonne*), and roasted potatoes.

Colorful carrot soup precedes the main course of tender beef, browned bacon, carrots, and mushrooms in red wine sauce. For maximum ease, serve the sauté on a large platter and let your guests help themselves. Crisp broccoli completes the meal.

Carrot Soup
Boeuf Bourguignon Sauté
Butter-Braised Broccoli

French thrift has inspired some of the world's great soups. This one is best prepared with large mature carrots, sometimes called "cooking" carrots, which have a rich flavor. If you can find only slender young carrots, use one or two extra, and accent their flavor with a pinch or two of sugar.

Selecting beautiful broccoli is simple: Look for firm, bright green heads with compact buds. Avoid any that have yellowed—a sure sign of age. Refrigerate unwashed broccoli in a plastic bag. It will keep for several days.

WHAT TO DRINK

The right drink here is a medium-bodied red wine from southern Burgundy—a Mercurey, for instance, or a Beaujolais Villages. A California, Washington, or Oregon Pinot Noir would also make a fine accompaniment.

SHOPPING LIST AND STAPLES

1½ pounds boneless top sirloin steak or tenderloin,
   cut into 1½-inch cubes
½ pound slab bacon
2 bunches broccoli (about 1½ pounds total weight)
2 large "cooking" carrots plus 2 small young carrots,
   or 6 small carrots (about ¾ pound total weight)
1 small russet or new potato (about ¼ pound total weight)
1 large plus 1 small yellow onion
Small bunch celery
12 small mushrooms
2 medium-size shallots
Small bunch parsley (optional)
1¼ cups heavy cream
6 tablespoons unsalted butter
1 bay leaf
1 teaspoon dried thyme
Whole nutmeg, preferably, or ½ teaspoon ground,
   approximately
Salt
Freshly ground black pepper
Freshly ground white pepper
⅔ cup dry red wine, approximately

UTENSILS

Food processor or blender
Large, wide saucepan or sauté pan with cover
2 large saucepans, 1 with cover
Colander
Measuring cups and spoons
Chef's knife
Paring knife
2 metal spoons or metal tongs
Wooden spoon
Ladle
Vegetable peeler
Bulb baster (optional)
Nutmeg grater (optional)

START-TO-FINISH STEPS

1. Follow beef recipe steps 1 through 4 and soup recipe steps 1 through 5.
2. Follow beef recipe step 5 and broccoli recipe step 1.
3. Follow soup recipe steps 6 and 7, and broccoli recipe step 2.
4. While broccoli is braising, follow beef recipe step 6 and then broccoli recipe step 3.
5. Follow beef recipe steps 7 and 8, and broccoli recipe step 4.
6. Follow soup recipe steps 8 and 9, and beef recipe step 9.
7. Follow soup recipe step 10 and serve.
8. Follow beef recipe step 10 and serve with broccoli.

RECIPES
Carrot Soup

Small yellow onion
1 stalk celery
2 large "cooking" carrots or 4 small young carrots
Small russet or new potato
2 tablespoons unsalted butter
Whole nutmeg, preferably, or ½ teaspoon ground
1 teaspoon salt
Freshly ground white pepper
1¼ cups heavy cream, approximately

1. Preheat oven to 200 degrees.
2. Peel and thinly slice enough onion to measure about ⅓ cup. Wash, trim, and thinly slice celery. Peel and thinly slice carrots and potato.
3. In large saucepan, melt butter over medium heat. Add onion and celery, and cook, stirring occasionally, until onion is tender but not browned, 3 to 5 minutes.

4. Grate enough nutmeg to measure ½ teaspoon, if using whole.

5. Add carrots, potato, salt, ¼ teaspoon nutmeg, pepper to taste, and 3 cups water. Cover saucepan and bring to a boil over high heat. Reduce heat to low and simmer 8 to 10 minutes, or until carrots and potato are soft.

6. Place 4 bowls or soup plates in oven to warm.

7. Remove pan from heat, uncover, and allow vegetables to cool slightly.

8. Coarsely purée vegetables and liquid, in batches if necessary, in food processor or blender.

9. Return soup to saucepan and stir in cream, thinning to desired consistency. Reheat soup over low heat, and add additional salt, pepper, or nutmeg to taste.

10. Ladle soup into warmed bowls and serve.

Boeuf Bourguignon Sauté

Large yellow onion
Small bunch shallots
½ pound slab bacon
2 small carrots
12 small mushrooms
1½ pounds boneless top sirloin steak or tenderloin, cut into 1½-inch cubes
1 bay leaf
1 teaspoon thyme, crumbled
⅔ cup dry red wine, approximately
Salt and freshly ground black pepper
Small bunch parsley for garnish (optional)

1. Peel and chop onion. Peel and mince enough shallots to measure ¼ cup. Cut bacon into 1-inch squares.

2. In large, wide saucepan or sauté pan, cook bacon over medium heat until pan is well coated with fat. Add onion and shallots, and cook until bacon is almost crisp and onion is tender but not browned, about 5 minutes.

3. While bacon is cooking, peel carrots and cut into 2-inch lengths. Wipe mushrooms clean with damp paper towels; set aside.

4. Add carrots and beef to pan, and cook over medium-high heat, stirring occasionally, until meat is evenly browned, about 10 minutes.

5. When beef is browned, add bay leaf, thyme, wine, and salt and pepper to taste. Cover and simmer over low heat 10 to 12 minutes, until fragrant.

6. Wash parsley, if using, and pat dry. Chop enough to measure 1 tablespoon; set aside.

7. Add additional wine, if needed to keep meat moist, and gently stir in mushrooms. Cover and cook over low heat 5 minutes. Meat will be medium-rare to rare and carrots crisp-tender. Do not overcook meat.

8. Place serving platter in oven to warm.

9. Remove and discard bay leaf. With a spoon or bulb baster, skim off any visible fat. Remove sauté pan from heat and keep covered until ready to serve.

10. When ready to serve, turn beef and vegetables onto warm platter and serve garnished with chopped parsley, if desired.

Butter-Braised Broccoli

2 bunches broccoli (about 1½ pounds total weight)
3 tablespoons unsalted butter
Salt and freshly ground white pepper

1. Wash broccoli and do not dry. Cut off the florets, or flowery heads, leaving an inch or so of stem intact.

2. Place florets in large saucepan over medium heat. Add butter, cover, and braise 5 minutes in the water remaining on florets after washing, checking to see if broccoli is beginning to brown and adding 1 to 2 tablespoons water, if necessary. Sprinkle lightly with salt and pepper.

3. Reduce heat, cover, and continue cooking until broccoli is crisp yet tender, about 3 minutes longer.

4. Turn into heatproof serving bowl and keep warm in oven until ready to serve.

ADDED TOUCH

For this elegant dessert, choose the pear variety that suits your palate: Bell-shaped Bartletts have a mildly sweet flavor; plump Anjous are rich and spicy; and slender Boscs are usually slightly acidic.

Pears Poached in Vanilla Syrup

¾ cup sugar
1 teaspoon vanilla extract
4 Bartlett, Anjou, or Bosc pears
½ cup crème fraîche (see recipe on page 72)

1. In large skillet, bring 2 cups water and sugar to a boil over high heat, stirring until sugar is dissolved. Boil 2 minutes, add vanilla extract, and keep syrup at boiling point.

2. One at a time, peel pears and core from bottom, leaving stems intact. (It is almost impossible to remove the complete core, but use a sharp knife or apple corer to scoop out as much of it as possible). If necessary, trim bottoms of pears flat, so they will stand firmly upright.

3. Using tongs, dip each pear in boiling syrup to coat well and prevent darkening, and turn pear on its side in syrup.

4. After all pears have been added to skillet, test the first one for doneness by piercing it with the tip of a small knife or a skewer. If tender, remove with tongs, holding briefly over skillet to drain. As each pear is done, remove from syrup, drain, and place upright in serving dish.

5. Raise heat under skillet to high and cook syrup until reduced by half, about 15 minutes. Pour syrup around pears in serving dish, cover loosely with foil or plastic wrap, and refrigerate at least 30 minutes or until ready to serve.

6. Divide cold pears among individual dessert plates and serve topped with a generous spoonful of crème fraîche.

LEFTOVER SUGGESTION

Peel leftover broccoli stems and slice them thinly for stir frying or to use as a garnish for soups or salads. Also, steamed, peeled, and diced broccoli stems are a delicious addition to omelets and quiches.

Chicken Liver and Lettuce Salad
Game Hens in Claret
Cauliflower au Gratin

Serve the chicken liver salad before or with the main course of Rock Cornish game hens and cauliflower au gratin.

The first-course salad is an adaptation of a Gascon dish that calls for warm goose or duck livers. For her version, Jeanne Voltz uses chicken livers, cooked briefly so they remain tender and juicy. Instead of Romaine, you may want to try radicchio or arugula. For a more highly seasoned salad, add minced garlic to taste.

The red Bordeaux used in the sauce for the hens is called claret—the traditional English name for the light red wines of Bordeaux.

WHAT TO DRINK

This menu is ideal for either light red or big white wines. For red, choose a Bordeaux wine, such as a Margaux or Saint-Émilion, which you can also use for the sauce for the game hens. For white, a California Chardonnay or a *premier cru* Chablis would be a good choice.

SHOPPING LIST AND STAPLES

2 Rock Cornish game hens (about 1¼ pounds each), with backbone removed, split, and flattened
½ pound chicken livers
¼ pound bacon (approximately 4 slices)
½ pound medium-size mushrooms
Large head cauliflower (about 1½ pounds)
Small yellow onion
Small head Bibb or Boston lettuce
1 head Romaine
½ pint heavy cream
2 tablespoons lightly salted butter
2 ounces Gruyère cheese
2 ounces Parmesan cheese
1 tablespoon olive oil
2 tablespoons red wine vinegar
1 tablespoon Dijon mustard
2 teaspoons sugar
1 slice stale white bread
½ teaspoon dried thyme
Salt
Freshly ground black pepper
Freshly ground white pepper
½ cup Margaux or other red Bordeaux wine, approximately

UTENSILS

Food processor or blender
2 large heavy-gauge skillets
Large saucepan with cover
9 x 13-inch baking dish
Small bowl
Colander
Salad spinner (optional)
Measuring cups and spoons
Chef's knife
Boning knife (optional)
Paring knife

Metal spoon or wooden spoon
Wide metal spatula
Metal tongs
Poultry shears (optional)
Grater (if not using food processor)

START-TO-FINISH STEPS

1. Follow game hens recipe steps 1 through 3 and salad recipe steps 1 and 2.
2. Turn game hens and follow cauliflower recipe steps 1 through 4.
3. Follow game hens recipe steps 4 and 5, and cauliflower recipe steps 5 and 6.
4. Check game hens periodically, turning and adjusting heat as needed. Follow salad recipe steps 3 and 4.
5. Follow cauliflower recipe steps 7 and 8.
6. Follow salad recipe steps 5 through 7, game hens recipe step 6, and serve with cauliflower.

RECIPES

Chicken Liver and Lettuce Salad

Small head Bibb or Boston lettuce
8 to 10 large leaves Romaine lettuce
¼ pound bacon (approximately 4 slices)
½ pound chicken livers
Small yellow onion
2 teaspoons sugar
1 tablespoon Dijon mustard
2 tablespoons red wine vinegar

1. Wash lettuce thoroughly and dry in salad spinner or pat dry with paper towels. Tear lettuce leaves into bite-size pieces and arrange on individual salad plates. Cover with plastic wrap and refrigerate.
2. Slice bacon into 1-inch squares and chicken livers into 1-inch cubes. Peel and mince onion.
3. In a large heavy-gauge skillet, cook bacon until almost crisp, about 3 minutes.
4. While bacon is cooking, rinse chicken livers under cold running water and pat dry with paper towels. Remove membranes; set aside.
5. Add onion and chicken livers, and cook, stirring often, until livers are browned but still tender, about 4 minutes.
6. Add sugar and mustard, and stir well. Add vinegar, carefully pouring it down side of skillet to avoid splattering, and cook mixture, stirring, about 2 minutes, or until bubbly.
7. Divide liver mixture among salad plates and top with sauce. Serve while still warm.

Game Hens in Claret

2 Rock Cornish game hens (about 1¼ pounds each), with backbone removed, split, and flattened
½ pound medium-size mushrooms
2 tablespoons unsalted butter

1 tablespoon olive oil
½ teaspoon dried thyme
1 teaspoon salt
Freshly ground black pepper
½ cup Margaux or other red Bordeaux wine

1. In a few minutes you can easily bone, split, and flatten game hens yourself. Remove giblets and necks from hens, and refrigerate for another use. With poultry shears, cut down each side of backbone from tail to neck, splitting hen in half; discard backbone. Flatten halves of hen on countertop or cutting board and, with paring knife, cut through breast, slit membrane over breast bone, and remove it. With the heel of your hand, press halves flat again.
2. Wipe mushrooms clean with damp towels; set aside.
3. In 1 or 2 large heavy-gauge skillets, melt butter with oil over medium-high heat. With skin sides down, sauté game hens until golden, about 5 minutes. Turn and sauté another 5 minutes.
4. Sprinkle with thyme, salt, and pepper to taste. Add mushrooms to skillet, and stir until thoroughly coated with pan juices.
5. Add wine and cook 15 to 25 minutes, or until liquid is almost absorbed and game hens are tender but not dry.
6. Divide hens among individual plates and top with pan juices and mushrooms.

Cauliflower au Gratin

Large head cauliflower (about 1½ pounds)
½ teaspoon salt
1 slice stale white bread
2 ounces Gruyère cheese
2 ounces Parmesan cheese
½ cup heavy cream
Freshly ground white pepper

1. Preheat oven to 450 degrees. Generously butter shallow rectangular baking dish.
2. Cut off leaves and remove core from cauliflower. Break or cut head into small florets; reserve core and leaves for another use.
3. In large saucepan, combine florets, salt, and ½ cup water and bring to a boil over high heat. Reduce heat to medium and cook, covered, until crisp-tender, about 7 minutes. Check cauliflower and add more hot water, if needed, to prevent burning.
4. In food processor or blender, finely grind the stale bread. Measure out 2 tablespoons of crumbs, place in small bowl, and set aside.
5. In food processor or with grater, shred enough Gruyère to measure ¼ cup and grate enough Parmesan to measure 2 tablespoons. Combine Parmesan and bread crumbs.
6. Transfer cauliflower to colander, refresh under cold running water, and drain.
7. Arrange cauliflower, with florets facing up, in baking dish. Sprinkle with Gruyère, carefully drizzle with cream, and season with white pepper to taste. Sprinkle evenly with bread crumb-Parmesan mixture.

8. Place dish on top rack of oven and bake about 10 minutes, or until sauce is bubbly and top is lightly browned.

ADDED TOUCH

Vanilla sugar, prepared in advance and kept as a kitchen staple, imparts a delicious flavor when used in cooking desserts or when sprinkled on fresh fruits. Spoon about one and three-quarters cups of confectioners' sugar (or granulated sugar, if preferred) into a quart jar with screw-top lid. Push a vanilla bean into the sugar, breaking bean, if necessary, to fit in jar. Cover and let stand at room temperature about three weeks before using. Replenish by adding more sugar as long as vanilla bean retains its flavor.

Caramel Apples with Vanilla Cream

3 tablespoons lightly salted butter
4 to 6 apples, such as Golden Delicious, Granny Smith, or McIntosh (about 1½ to 2 pounds total weight)
⅓ cup sugar, approximately
2 tablespoons brandy, Calvados, or Applejack
Vanilla Cream (see following recipe)

1. In large cast-iron skillet, melt butter, tipping skillet to coat evenly. Turn off heat, but leave skillet on burner to keep hot.
2. One at a time, peel, core, and slice enough apples into ¼-inch-thick wedges to measure about 5½ cups. As they are cut, place apple slices in skillet and turn with metal tongs to coat with butter.
3. When all apples have been prepared and coated with butter, spread into a thin layer in skillet. Turn heat to high and cook about 4 minutes, or until apples appear tinged with gold, turning gently with a wide spatula once or twice.
4. Sprinkle with sugar to taste, depending on sweetness of apples, and continue cooking until juices running from apples are almost evaporated.
5. Remove skillet from heat and sprinkle apples with brandy. Return skillet to burner, bring liquid to a fast boil, and cook about 3 minutes, or until juices are syrupy but apples still retain their shape.
6. Turn into serving bowl, cover, and let stand at room temperature until ready to serve. Or refrigerate overnight and reheat before serving.
7. To serve, divide among dessert bowls and top with Vanilla Cream.

Vanilla Cream

½ cup heavy cream
½ cup sour cream
1 tablespoon vanilla sugar, approximately

1. In small bowl, combine heavy cream, sour cream, and vanilla sugar to taste, and stir until blended.
2. Cover and let stand 1 to 2 hours at room temperature, or refrigerate until 30 minutes before serving. Serve at room temperature.

Mushrooms with Snail Butter
Broiled Butterflied Leg of Lamb in Red Wine
Crock-Roasted Potatoes

Mushrooms filled with snail, or seasoned, butter and roasted potatoes accompany the succulent lamb.

Broiled butterflied leg of lamb, seasoned with rosemary and red wine, is an elegant main dish for a company meal. A "butterflied" leg has had the bones and fat removed. Its thick parts are cut so that the meat can be opened out as if it were hinged (resembling a butterfly's wings), then the meat is spread out and pounded flat for broiling.

French cooks often roast potatoes on the stove-top in an earthenware crock, but you can use a heavy cast-iron pot instead. Covered tightly, the potatoes cook slowly without liquid, roasting in their own juices. When they are done, a rich potato aroma permeates the kitchen.

WHAT TO DRINK

The Pommard called for in the lamb recipe would be ideal served along with the entrée. As an alternative, you could select a good Saint-Émilion or Médoc from a small château.

SHOPPING LIST AND STAPLES

2½ pounds butterflied leg of lamb
12 large mushrooms with 2- to 3-inch-wide caps (about ¾ pound total weight)

8 to 12 small russet potatoes (about 1½ pounds total weight)
4 to 6 large shallots
Small clove garlic plus 2 cloves (optional)
Small bunch rosemary (optional)
Small bunch parsley
4 tablespoons unsalted (or lightly salted, if preferred) plus 4 tablespoons unsalted butter
¼ cup chicken stock, preferably homemade (see page 11), or canned
1 teaspoon cornstarch
2 teaspoons dried rosemary
Salt
Freshly ground black pepper
1 cup dry red wine, such as Pommard or Médoc

UTENSILS

Small skillet
Small saucepan with cover
Large heavy-gauge flameproof casserole with tight-fitting cover
13 x 9 x 2-inch baking pan
Large shallow glass or ceramic dish
Serving platter
Small mixing bowl
Colander
Measuring cups and spoons
Chef's knife
Paring knife
2 metal spoons
Metal tongs
Fork
Pastry brush
Heat diffuser (optional)

START-TO-FINISH STEPS

1. Peel and mince shallots for mushrooms and for lamb. Peel and mince garlic for mushrooms. Follow lamb recipe step 1.
2. Follow potatoes recipe steps 1 and 2, and mushrooms recipe steps 1 and 2.
3. Follow lamb recipe steps 2 and 3.
4. Follow potatoes recipe step 3 and mushrooms recipe steps 3 through 5.
5. Follow lamb recipe steps 4 and 5, and mushrooms recipe step 6.
6. Follow lamb recipe steps 6 through 10 and mushrooms recipe step 7.
7. Follow lamb recipe steps 11 and 12, potatoes recipe step 4, and serve with mushrooms.

RECIPES

Mushrooms with Snail Butter

12 large mushrooms (about ¾ pound total weight)
Large sprig parsley

4 tablespoons unsalted butter
2 to 3 large shallots
Small clove garlic
¼ cup chicken stock

1. Wipe mushrooms clean with damp paper towels. Remove stems and reserve for another use. Wash parsley sprig and pat dry. Chop parsley.
2. In small bowl, break up butter with a fork. Sprinkle parsley, shallots, and garlic over butter. Set aside for at least 15 minutes to allow butter to soften and absorb flavors.
3. In small saucepan, heat chicken stock over low heat. Add mushrooms, cover, and simmer 3 to 4 minutes, or until mushrooms are just tender.
4. While mushrooms simmer, rapidly mix butter with seasonings.
5. With tongs, remove mushrooms from stock and place on paper towels to drain.
6. Arrange mushrooms, with gill sides up, in shallow baking pan. Spoon 1 teaspoon seasoned butter into each cap.
7. Broil mushrooms 4 to 5 inches from heating element about 5 minutes, or until butter is bubbly and mushrooms are heated through.

Broiled Butterflied Leg of Lamb in Red Wine

2½ pounds butterflied leg of lamb
1 cup dry red wine, such as Pommard or Médoc
2 to 3 large shallots, peeled and minced
2 teaspoons dried rosemary
Salt
Freshly ground pepper
1 teaspoon cornstarch
French rosemary sprigs for garnish (optional)

1. To marinate lamb, place fat side down in large shallow glass or ceramic dish. Pour wine over meat and sprinkle with shallots and dried rosemary. Turn meat and let stand at room temperature 15 to 30 minutes, turning once or twice.
2. Grease tray or rack of broiler pan well to facilitate clean-up. Preheat broiler.
3. If using rosemary for garnish, wash and pat dry with paper towels.
4. Using tongs, lift lamb from marinade and place fat side up on broiler pan tray or rack. Reserve marinade for sauce.
5. Broil lamb 4 to 5 inches from heating element 8 to 10 minutes, or until well browned.
6. Brush meat with marinade, turn, and brush other side. Broil another 10 to 15 minutes, or until well browned. The thick parts should be rare and thinner sections medium to well done.
7. Place platter under hot running water.
8. Dry platter. Transfer lamb to warm platter and cover loosely with foil.
9. Skim most of fat from drippings and pour drippings into small skillet. Add reserved marinade and bring to a boil over high heat. Season with salt and pepper to taste.

10. Place dinner plates under hot running water to warm.
11. Blend cornstarch with 1 tablespoon of water into a paste. Add cornstarch paste to marinade and cook, stirring, 3 to 5 minutes, or until slightly thickened and smooth.
12. Dry plates. Slice lamb and divide among dinner plates. Top with sauce and serve garnished with rosemary sprigs, if desired.

Crock-Roasted Potatoes

8 to 12 small russet potatoes (about 1½ pounds total weight)
2 cloves garlic (optional)
4 tablespoons unsalted butter (or lightly salted, if preferred)

1. Wash potatoes. In *very heavy*-gauge casserole with *tight-fitting* cover, arrange potatoes in single layer. Place unpeeled garlic in pot. Cover pan, fitting sheet of aluminum foil or cooking parchment between pot and lid, if necessary, to make a very tight seal.
2. Using a heat diffuser or spreader on cooking surface if needed to produce slow, even heat, place pan over very low heat. Cook potatoes, without adding any liquid, 15 minutes.
3. Using a pot holder, lift cover and use metal tongs to turn potatoes. Do not puncture them. Cover and cook until potatoes are very tender, about 30 minutes.
4. Divide among individual plates and dot with butter.

ADDED TOUCH

For an elegant summer dessert, use fully ripe, juicy, and fragrant freestone peaches. The coarse peach purée gives texture to the dessert. If you cannot find fresh raspberries for the sauce, substitute frozen ones.

Peach Bavarian Cream with Raspberry Sauce

1½ pounds peaches or unsweetened frozen peaches, or Bartlett, Bosc, or Anjou pears (about 1 cup puréed)
1 tablespoon freshly squeezed lemon juice
4 egg yolks plus 3 egg whites
1 envelope unflavored gelatin
⅓ cup sugar, approximately
½ cup milk
½ cup heavy cream
Raspberry Sauce (see following recipe)

1. In large saucepan, bring 2 quarts of water to a boil. Submerge peaches in boiling water and blanch 30 seconds. Drain, peel, pit, and slice peaches.
2. In food processor or blender, coarsely purée enough peaches to measure 1 cup. Immediately stir in lemon juice to prevent discoloration.
3. Separate egg yolks and whites (see illustration above), placing yolks in a small bowl, 3 whites in a mixing bowl, and reserving 1 egg white for another use.
4. In top of double boiler or in bowl that can be fitted over

1. Crack egg against side of bowl.

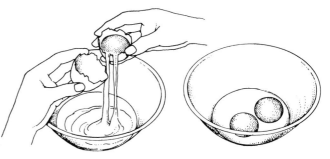

2. Separate each egg by pouring back and forth between halves of shell until the entire white has dropped into one bowl.

but not sit in a pan of water, combine gelatin, ⅓ cup sugar, egg yolks, and milk. Add more sugar if peaches are not sweet enough.
5. Place egg mixture over hot water on very low heat and cook, stirring, 3 to 5 minutes, or until thickened and smooth.
6. Cool mixture by setting bowl in large container of cold water for about 15 minutes. Stir in peach purée. Chill in refrigerator until thickened but not set, about 30 minutes.
7. Beat egg whites until stiff but not dry. Fold gently into peach mixture. In another bowl, whip cream and fold into peaches.
8. Rinse a 1½-quart mold in cold water, then turn mixture into mold. Cover and chill overnight or until set, 6 to 8 hours.
9. When ready to serve, unmold Bavarian onto serving plate and top with a few spoonfuls of raspberry sauce. Serve remaining sauce separately.

Raspberry Sauce

1 pint fresh raspberries
3 to 4 tablespoons granulated sugar or vanilla sugar
½ teaspoon vanilla extract (omit if using vanilla sugar)

1. Gently rinse raspberries and spread on paper towels to drain.
2. Press raspberries through food mill or strainer set over small bowl to purée pulp and remove seeds.
3. Stir 3 tablespoons sugar and vanilla or vanilla sugar only into purée. Add more sugar to taste. Cover and refrigerate sauce until ready to serve.

LEFTOVER SUGGESTION

Use the mushroom stems in a vegetable soup, or mince them finely and mix with grated cheese as a filling for an omelet. Use leftover snail butter to season broiled meat, or spread on toasted French bread.

Leslee Reis

Leslee Reis has traveled often in Alsace and throughout France—but not as an ordinary tourist might. She prefers to visit local farmers, marketplaces, and small unstarred (or perhaps one-starred) restaurants and enjoys observing the terrain and the character of the local people. Her three menus are taken from Alsace and Provence, but she has tailored them to the American marketplace.

Menu 1 is Alsatian. The first-course salad is an adaptation of the famous Alsatian one-course meal *choucroute garnie,* or braised sauerkraut garnished with pieces of pork, salt pork, sausage, or bacon. The entrée also features two other specialties of the region: pork, here in the form of sausages, and Riesling, the celebrated white wine, which is used in the sauce.

Menus 2 and 3 are Provence-inspired. In Menu 2, Leslee Reis has created a fish stew that resembles the *bouillabaisse* of Marseilles. Menu 3 features artichokes braised in olive oil with basil and garlic—a combination typical of the region, as is the union of tomato and garlic, used here for an interesting variation of *coquilles St. Jacques.*

Chicken pieces, sliced garlic sausages, and chopped vegetables are heaped on a bed of golden egg noodles for this Alsatian dinner. For the salad, serve individual portions of sauerkraut on curly lettuce leaves, surrounded by walnuts, cornichons, *lardoons, and onions.*

Choucroute Salad
Chicken and Sausages in Riesling Sauce with Egg Noodles

Choucroute, or sauerkraut, a ubiquitous ingredient in Alsatian cooking, is white cabbage that has been finely shredded, salted, and then left to ferment. Pork and mustard are its classic partners; here the cook suggests salt pork and Dijon mustard. The pork is cut into lardoons, or strips, then blanched and fried. Blanching the pork strips tempers their saltiness so that the pork does not overwhelm the onions, walnuts, and *cornichons* (small sour French pickles) in the salad.

Alsatian Riesling, a major flavoring in the sauce for the chicken and sausages, is a dry, crisp white wine that complements seafood, poultry, sauerkraut, and pork, and is less sweet than the German or California Rieslings.

WHAT TO DRINK

The cook suggests an Alsatian Riesling or Pinot Blanc to go with the *choucroute* salad in this menu. A New York State, Oregon, or California Riesling would also be good choices.

SHOPPING LIST AND STAPLES

3-pound broiler-fryer, cut into 8 pieces
1 pound fresh garlic sausages
½ pound lean salt pork
Large turnip
Large onion
2 medium-size carrots
Small bunch celery
1 head soft lettuce, preferably leaf or Boston
½ pint heavy cream
½ to ¾ pound ½-inch-wide egg noodles, preferably fresh, or dried
2 cups sauerkraut, preferably fresh, or 16-ounce bag
2 cups chicken stock, preferably homemade (see page 11), or canned
5 tablespoons vegetable oil, approximately
5 tablespoons walnut oil, preferably, or peanut oil
¼ cup peanut oil, plus another 5 tablespoons if not using walnut oil
¼ cup red wine vinegar
½ teaspoon Dijon mustard, preferably coarse- grained
7-ounce jar cornichons
3½-ounce package walnut pieces
Salt and freshly ground pepper
1 cup Alsatian Riesling wine

UTENSILS

Stockpot
Large deep ovenproof skillet with cover
Small skillet
Medium-size saucepan
10 x 15-inch cookie sheet
Platter
Medium-size bowl
Small bowl
Colander
Salad spinner (optional)
Measuring cups and spoons
Chef's knife
Paring knife
Slotted spoon
Wooden spoon

START-TO-FINISH STEPS

1. Follow salad recipe step 1.
2. Peel and dice onion. Follow chicken and sausages recipe steps 1 through 5.
3. Follow salad recipe steps 2 through 7.
4. Follow chicken and sausages recipe steps 6 through 8.
5. While water for pasta is coming to a boil, follow salad recipe steps 8 and 9, and serve as first course.
6. Follow chicken and sausages recipe steps 9 and 10, and serve.

RECIPES

Choucroute Salad

½ pound lean salt pork
¼ cup peanut oil, plus another 5 tablespoons if not using walnut oil
½ cup walnut pieces
5 tablespoons walnut oil, preferably, or peanut oil
Salt
2 cups sauerkraut, preferably fresh, or prepared
1 head soft lettuce, preferably leaf or Boston
½ cup cornichons
¼ cup red wine vinegar
½ teaspoon Dijon mustard, preferably coarse-grained
¼ teaspoon freshly ground pepper
¼ cup diced onion

1. Preheat oven to 400 degrees.

2. Cut salt pork into lardoons (¼-inch-thick, 1½-inch-long julienne). In medium-size saucepan, bring 1 quart water to a boil over high heat. Add lardoons and blanch 1 minute. Transfer to colander and rinse under cold running water. Drain and pat dry with paper towels.

3. In small skillet, heat 2 tablespoons peanut oil over medium heat. Add lardoons and cook, stirring occasionally to prevent burning, 3 to 5 minutes, or until browned. Remove with slotted spoon and drain on paper towels.

4. While lardoons are browning, chop walnuts.

5. In small bowl, mix walnuts with 1 tablespoon walnut or peanut oil and sprinkle with salt to taste. Arrange on cookie sheet in single layer and toast in oven 5 to 8 minutes, or just until brown. Reduce oven temperature to 200 degrees.

6. While walnuts are toasting, wash lettuce and dry in salad spinner or pat dry with paper towels. Wrap in paper towels and refrigerate until needed. Cut cornichons into ¼-inch-thick slices; set aside.

7. In colander, rinse sauerkraut under cold running water. Drain and pat dry with paper towels. Set aside.

8. For vinaigrette, combine ¼ cup walnut oil, if using, remaining 2 tablespoons peanut oil (or 6 tablespoons peanut oil if not using walnut oil), vinegar, mustard, ½ teaspoon salt; and pepper in medium-size bowl. Add sauerkraut and toss to coat.

9. Line 4 individual salad bowls with lettuce leaves. Top each with sauerkraut and surround with small portions of lardoons, walnuts, onion, and cornichons.

Chicken and Sausages in Riesling Sauce with Egg Noodles

1 pound fresh garlic sausages
3-pound broiler-fryer, cut into 8 pieces
5 tablespoons vegetable oil, approximately
½ cup diced onion
2 medium-size carrots
Large turnip
1 celery rib
1 cup Alsatian Riesling wine
2 cups chicken stock, preferably homemade (see page 11),
    or canned
½ teaspoon freshly ground pepper
¼ cup heavy cream
½ to ¾ pound ½-inch-wide egg noodles, preferably fresh,
    or dried
1 teaspoon salt

1. Slice sausages into ½-inch-thick rounds. Cut rounds into semicircles. In large deep ovenproof skillet, sauté sausages over medium heat only until skins are brown and fat is rendered, about 7 minutes. Remove sausages with slotted spoon and drain on paper towels. Reserve fat in skillet.

2. While sausages are browning, wash chicken pieces and pat dry with paper towels. Add to skillet and sauté over medium heat in sausage fat 5 to 7 minutes, turning to brown evenly. If necessary to prevent sticking, add 1 to 2 tablespoons vegetable oil. Transfer chicken to platter and set aside.

3. While chicken is browning, peel and dice carrots and turnip. Wash, trim, and dice celery.

4. Add onion, carrots, turnip, and celery to skillet, and sauté 2 to 3 minutes, or until soft. If necessary to prevent sticking, add 1 to 2 tablespoons vegetable oil.

5. Return chicken to skillet. Add wine, stock, and pepper, and bring to a boil. Lower heat, cover, and simmer until chicken is tender, 20 to 25 minutes.

6. Return sausages to skillet and simmer another 3 to 4 minutes.

7. Add cream to skillet and stir until blended. Simmer 1 to 2 minutes to marry the flavors. Remove pan from heat, cover, and keep warm in 200-degree oven. Place 4 dinner plates in oven to warm.

8. In stockpot, bring 4 quarts lightly salted water to a boil over high heat.

9. Add noodles to boiling water and cook 3 to 4 minutes for fresh, 8 to 12 minutes for dried. Transfer to colander and drain. Return noodles to pot and toss with 1 tablespoon vegetable oil.

10. Divide noodles among 4 warm dinner plates and top with chicken and sausages.

ADDED TOUCH

Alsatians love their beer almost as much as they love their own wine, and this dark-beer dessert will surprise and delight your palate. It is refreshing, with a taste that is difficult to identify immediately. It is also very easy to make and can be prepared a day or two in advance, if desired.

Dark-Beer Granité

1 cup sugar
3 cups dark beer
1 tablespoon fresh lemon juice

1. In the morning, open beer and allow to flatten.

2. In small heavy-gauge saucepan, combine sugar with 1 cup water and bring to a boil over medium heat. Reduce heat and cook, without stirring, 7 to 10 minutes, or until mixture turns a light caramel color.

3. Remove pan from heat. Add beer very slowly, stirring to combine. Return to heat and stir 2 to 3 minutes, or until smooth.

4. Remove pan from heat and stir in lemon juice. Pour into shallow 9 x 12-inch pan and allow to cool at least 15 minutes. Place in freezer.

5. After 30 to 40 minutes, "shave" the beer granité as follows: With a fork, scrape through it several times and return to freezer. After 30 minutes, shave it again. Repeat.

6. Beer granité is ready to serve when totally frozen but in shavings. Divide among balloon wine glasses or small bowls and serve immediately.

Marinated Vegetable Salad
Marseillaise Fish Stew with Rouille and Cheese Croutons

This flavorful fish stew is a simple version of *bouillabaisse*, which contains many varieties of fish and shellfish. Here only one type of firm-fleshed fish and mussels are used. The stew is served with *rouille*, a peppery mayonnaise-like sauce.

WHAT TO DRINK

A good wine for this menu would be a dry rosé such as Tavel or a firm, clean Muscadet.

To accentuate the colors and textures of the fish stew, serve it in a large tureen with the rouille *in a separate bowl and a marinated green bean, mushroom, and red pepper salad on the side. Keep the cheese croutons warm in a napkin-lined basket.*

SHOPPING LIST AND STAPLES

1½ pounds fillets of firm-fleshed non-oily fish, such as bass, snapper, grouper, cod, or halibut
1 pound mussels (about 20), cleaned and beards removed
2 leeks
1 fennel bulb (about 1 pound)
Medium-size onion
½ pound green beans
12 to 16 medium-size mushrooms
Red bell pepper
1 head Boston lettuce
3 medium-size tomatoes (about 1 pound total weight)
Small bunch parsley
Small bunch basil (optional)

Large head garlic
1 lemon
2 cups fish stock or two 8-ounce bottles clam juice
4-ounce jar pimiento
2 eggs
4 tablespoons unsalted butter
2 ounces Parmesan cheese
1 loaf French bread, preferably day-old
⅓ cup fresh bread crumbs
1¼ cups extra-virgin olive oil
½ teaspoon Dijon mustard
Hot pepper sauce
1 strip dried orange peel
1 teaspoon dried thyme
Pinch of saffron threads
Paprika
Salt
Freshly ground white and black pepper
2 cups dry white wine or vermouth

UTENSILS

Food processor or mortar and pestle
Large deep skillet with cover, or large heavy-gauge
    saucepan with cover
Large saucepan

10 x 15-inch cookie sheet
Medium-size bowl
2 small bowls plus additional small bowl (if not using
    processor)
Colander
Salad spinner (optional)
Measuring cups and spoons
Chef's knife
Paring knife
Slotted spoon
2 wooden spoons
Fork
Ladle

START-TO-FINISH STEPS

1. Prepare garlic for salad, stew, and rouille.
2. Follow stew recipe steps 1 through 4.
3. Follow salad recipe steps 1 through 6.
4. Follow croutons recipe steps 1 through 3.
5. Follow rouille recipe steps 1 through 6.
6. Follow salad recipe step 7.
7. Follow stew recipe steps 5 and 6.
8. Follow croutons recipe step 4 and salad recipe step 8.
9. Follow stew recipe steps 7 through 9 and serve with salad and croutons.

Marinated Vegetable Salad

Salt
½ pound green beans
12 to 16 medium-size mushrooms
½ red bell pepper
1 head Boston lettuce
2 cloves garlic, peeled and crushed
½ teaspoon freshly ground black pepper
½ teaspoon Dijon mustard
Juice of 1 lemon
½ cup plus 2 tablespoons extra-virgin olive oil

1. In large saucepan bring 2 quarts lightly salted water to a boil over high heat.
2. While water is heating, remove strings and trim stem ends of green beans.
3. Add beans to boiling water and cook 6 to 7 minutes, or until tender but still crisp.
4. While beans are cooking, wipe mushrooms clean with damp paper towels. Cut into ⅛-inch-thick slices. Wash bell pepper and pat dry. Cut into ¼-inch-thick strips. Wash lettuce and dry in salad spinner or pat dry with paper towels. Wrap in paper towels and refrigerate.
5. Transfer beans to colander, refresh under cold running water, and drain.
6. For vinaigrette, combine garlic, 1 teaspoon salt, pepper, mustard, lemon juice, and oil in medium-size bowl.
7. Fifteen minutes before serving, add beans, mushrooms, and bell pepper to vinaigrette, and toss gently.
8. Divide lettuce among four salad plates and top with marinated vegetables.

Marseillaise Fish Stew

2 leeks
1 fennel bulb (about 1 pound)
Small bunch parsley
Medium-size onion
2 tablespoons extra-virgin olive oil
3 cloves garlic, peeled and chopped
1 teaspoon dried thyme
1 strip dried orange peel
3 medium-size tomatoes (about 1 pound total weight)
2 cups dry white wine or vermouth
2 cups fish stock or two 8-ounce bottles clam juice
Pinch of saffron threads
Salt and freshly ground white pepper
1½ pounds fillets of firm-fleshed non-oily fish, such as bass, snapper, grouper, cod, halibut, etc.
1 pound mussels (about 20), cleaned and beards removed
Rouille (see following recipe)

1. Trim root ends and upper leaves of leeks, and split leeks lengthwise. Gently spread leaves and rinse under cold running water. Pat dry with paper towels. Cut into ½-inch-thick semicircles. Cut fennel bulb in half and slice into ½-inch-thick pieces. Wash parsley and pat dry. Chop enough parsley to measure ½ cup. Peel and chop onion.
2. In large deep nonaluminum skillet, heat olive oil over medium heat. Add leeks, fennel, and onion, and sauté 1 minute. Add ¼ cup parsley, garlic, thyme, and orange peel, and sauté another 5 minutes, or until tender.
3. Meanwhile, peel, core, seed, and chop tomatoes.
4. Add tomatoes, white wine, stock, saffron, and two cups water, and bring to a boil over high heat. Reduce heat to low and simmer, covered, 30 minutes. Season with salt and white pepper to taste.
5. Cut fish into portion-size pieces. Add fish to simmering broth and poach 8 to 10 minutes per 1-inch thickness.
6. Five minutes before fish should be done, add mussels to skillet and cook, covered, 5 minutes, or until mussels open. Discard any mussels that do not open.
7. Transfer fish and mussels with a slotted spoon to a tureen.
8. Taste broth, adjust seasoning, and ladle enough broth over fish to barely cover. Garnish with chopped parsley.
9. Stir rouille into remaining broth and pour into small bowl or sauceboat.

Rouille

4-ounce jar pimiento
3 cloves garlic, peeled and crushed
1 large fresh basil leaf (optional)
2 eggs
⅓ cup fresh bread crumbs
½ cup extra-virgin olive oil
Hot pepper sauce
Salt and freshly ground black pepper

1. Rinse, drain, and chop enough pimiento to measure 2 tablespoons.
2. Using food processor or a mortar and pestle, purée pimiento, garlic, and basil, if using, until paste-like but not completely smooth.
3. Separate eggs, adding 1½ yolks to garlic "paste" and reserving whites for another use.
4. Add bread crumbs and process another 5 seconds or turn mixture into a small bowl and blend with a spoon.
5. With processor running or while stirring, slowly drizzle in olive oil, as for mayonnaise, and continue to blend until mixture is thick and smooth.
6. Add hot pepper sauce and salt and pepper to taste, and stir to blend. Rouille should be very spicy.

Cheese Croutons

3 tablespoons freshly grated Parmesan cheese
4 tablespoons unsalted butter, at room temperature
1 loaf French bread, preferably day-old
Paprika

1. Preheat oven to 350 degrees.
2. In small bowl, blend cheese and butter with fork.
3. Cut bread into 12 slices. Spread one side of each slice with cheese-butter mixture and arrange slices in a single layer on cookie sheet. Sprinkle tops lightly with paprika.
4. Bake 8 to 10 minutes, or until crisp and golden.

Braised Artichoke Hearts with Fresh Basil
Coquilles St. Jacques Provençal / Buttered New Potatoes
Mixed Green Salad with Garlic Toast

This elegant meal for family or company features scallops in a tomato sauce, braised artichokes with leeks and fresh basil, and new potatoes. Garnish the mixed green salad of leaf lettuce, watercress, and radicchio with garlic toast triangles.

For the braised artichokes, you may prefer to use fresh artichoke bottoms. Buy small artichokes that are not opened or discolored. To prepare artichokes for cooking, wash them by plunging them into cold water, stems up, then snap off the stems and pull off any tough leaves from around the base. Slice off the top third of each artichoke. Cook the artichokes in boiling water for 15 to 45 minutes, depending on size, or until tender, then drain thoroughly. When the artichokes are cool, pull out the center leaves, scoop out the fuzzy choke with a teaspoon and remove all of the remaining leaves (reserve them to eat at a later time). You are left with artichoke bottoms.

WHAT TO DRINK

Either a white Burgundy, such as a Mâcon or Saint-Véran, or a dry California rosé would be fine here. Muscadet, from the Loire, is also a good choice.

SHOPPING LIST AND STAPLES

1½ pounds fresh sea scallops
8 small new potatoes (about 1¼ pounds total weight)
4 large tomatoes (about 2½ pounds total weight)
2 leeks
Medium-size onion
1 head radicchio
1 head Boston lettuce
1 head red-leaf lettuce
2 bunches watercress
Small bunch fresh parsley
Small bunch fresh basil, or ½ teaspoon dried
Small bunch fresh thyme, or 1½ teaspoons dried
2 heads garlic
1 stick unsalted butter
2 tablespoons chicken stock, preferably homemade (see page 11), or canned
9-ounce package frozen artichoke hearts
1 cup extra-virgin olive oil, approximately
¼ cup red wine vinegar
1 teaspoon Dijon mustard
Small loaf very thinly sliced white bread
2 bay leaves
Salt
Freshly ground pepper
1 cup dry white wine or ⅔ cup dry vermouth

UTENSILS

Medium-size heavy-gauge casserole or saucepan
 with cover
Large skillet
Medium-size saucepan
Small heavy-gauge saucepan or butter warmer
10 x 15-inch cookie sheet
Large salad bowl
Medium-size bowl
Small bowl
Colander
Salad spinner (optional)
Measuring cups and spoons
Chef's knife
Paring knife
Wooden spoon
Slotted spoon
Whisk
Pastry brush

START-TO-FINISH STEPS

1. Wash lettuce, watercress, radicchio, parsley, and fresh herbs, if using. Dry in salad spinner or pat dry with paper towels. Shred Boston lettuce for artichokes recipe and chop parsley for scallops recipe. Wrap watercress, leaf lettuce, and radicchio in paper towels and refrigerate until ready to assemble salad.
2. Follow artichokes recipe steps 1 through 4.
3. Follow scallop recipe steps 1 through 4 and artichokes recipe step 5.
4. Follow potatoes recipe steps 1 and 2, and scallops recipe steps 5 and 6.
5. Follow salad recipe steps 1 through 3.
6. Follow artichokes recipe steps 6 and 7, and potatoes recipe steps 3 and 4.
7. Follow salad recipe steps 4 and 5.
8. Follow scallops recipe step 7, salad recipe step 6, and serve with artichokes and potatoes.

RECIPES

Braised Artichoke Hearts with Fresh Basil

2 leeks
3 tablespoons unsalted butter
3 tablespoons extra-virgin olive oil

9-ounce package frozen artichoke hearts
6 cloves garlic, unpeeled
6 large leaves fresh basil, or ½ teaspoon dried
1 cup firmly packed coarsely shredded Boston lettuce
1 bay leaf
Salt and freshly ground pepper
1 to 2 tablespoons chicken stock

1. Trim off root ends of leeks, split lengthwise, and wash thoroughly. Trim off green leaves. Slice white part into ¼-inch semicircles.
2. In heavy-gauge casserole or saucepan, heat 2 tablespoons butter and oil over medium heat. Add leeks, artichoke hearts, and garlic, and cook, covered, 5 minutes, gently separating frozen artichoke hearts and turning to keep them from browning.
3. While vegetables are sweating, slice basil leaves into fine shreds. Reserve 2 sliced basil leaves for garnish.
4. Add basil, lettuce, bay leaf, and salt and pepper to taste to casserole. Cover, reduce heat to low, and cook very gently, stirring occasionally to prevent sticking, 20 to 25 minutes, or until artichokes are tender. If dish becomes too dry during braising, add 1 to 2 tablespoons chicken stock.
5. Place dinner plates under hot running water to warm.
6. Taste mixture and adjust seasoning, if necessary. Remove and discard bay leaf.
7. Remove casserole from heat and swirl in remaining tablespoon of butter to enrich the sauce. Divide among dinner plates and garnish with reserved basil.

Coquilles St. Jacques Provençal

Medium-size onion
4 cloves garlic
1½ pounds fresh sea scallops
Salt and freshly ground pepper
4 tablespoons extra-virgin olive oil
4 large tomatoes (about 2½ pounds total weight)
¼ cup chopped parsley
1½ tablespoons fresh thyme leaves or 1½ teaspoons dried
1 bay leaf
1 cup dry white wine or ⅔ cup dry vermouth

1. Peel and dice onion. Peel and finely mince garlic.
2. In colander, rinse scallops under cold running water. Pat dry with paper towels. Slice scallops horizontally in half and season with salt and pepper.

44

3. In large skillet, heat 2 tablespoons olive oil over medium heat. Add scallops and sauté quickly, just until opaque, about 2 minutes. Using slotted spoon, transfer scallops to medium-size bowl.
4. Add remaining olive oil to skillet and return to medium heat. Add onions and garlic, and sauté gently about 5 minutes, or until tender.
5. Core, peel, seed, and chop tomatoes.
6. Add tomatoes, parsley, thyme, bay leaf, wine, and accumulated juices from scallops to onion mixture. Cook, stirring occasionally, over medium-high heat, about 15 minutes, or until thickened and slightly reduced.
7. Add scallops to tomato mixture and cook just until heated through. Taste and adjust seasoning. Divide among dinner plates.

Buttered New Potatoes

8 small new potatoes (about 1¼ pounds total weight)
Salt
2 tablespoons unsalted butter
Freshly ground pepper

1. Scrub potatoes clean, leaving skins on.
2. Place potatoes in medium-size saucepan. Add 1 teaspoon salt and water to cover, and bring to a boil over medium-high heat. Lower heat to medium and continue boiling 20 minutes, or until potato may be pierced easily with a knife tip.
3. Transfer potatoes to colander and drain.
4. Off heat, add butter to the saucepan and, when butter is melted, add potatoes. Tilt and swirl pan to coat potatoes evenly. Add salt and pepper to taste. Cover and keep warm until ready to serve.

Mixed Green Salad with Garlic Toast

3 tablespoons unsalted butter
8 slices very thinly sliced white bread
6 large cloves garlic
½ teaspoon salt
Freshly ground pepper
1 teaspoon Dijon mustard
¼ cup red wine vinegar
½ cup extra-virgin olive oil
1 head radicchio
2 bunches watercress
1 head red-leaf lettuce

1. Preheat oven to 325 degrees.
2. In small heavy-gauge saucepan or butter warmer, melt butter over low heat.
3. Remove crusts from bread and cut each slice on the diagonal into two triangles. Brush cookie sheet with some of the melted butter and arrange bread triangles in a single layer on it. Brush tops of bread with remaining melted butter and dry in oven 10 to 15 minutes. Be careful not to burn bread. The toast may be made ahead and stored in an airtight container.
4. Remove toast from oven.
5. Peel garlic. In small bowl, mash 2 cloves. Add salt, pepper to taste, mustard, vinegar, and oil, and whisk until thoroughly blended. Set aside.
6. Place radicchio and greens in large salad bowl. Pour vinaigrette over salad and toss until evenly coated. Divide among 4 salad plates. Garnish each plate with 2 toast triangles and 1 whole garlic clove for rubbing toast.

ADDED TOUCH

Herbes de Provence is a mixture of dried herbs, such as lavender, thyme, rosemary, sage, and basil, that are frequently used in Provençal cooking and that are available prepackaged at specialty food shops. If you prefer, use fresh thyme alone to season this unusual dessert.

Poached Figs

1½ cups full-flavored red wine (Rhône, Zinfandel, Rioja)
3 tablespoons honey
½ teaspoon *herbes de Provence*, or 2 sprigs fresh thyme
12 fresh figs or ½ pound dried figs
¼ cup heavy cream

1. In medium-size saucepan, bring wine, honey, and herbs to a boil over high heat. Reduce heat and simmer 5 minutes.
2. Add figs, cover, and simmer gently until tender, 5 to 10 minutes for fresh, 15 to 20 minutes for dried.
3. With slotted spoon, transfer figs to large bowl.
4. Increase heat to high and reduce poaching liquid to a syrupy consistency, about 10 minutes. Pour over figs in bowl.
5. Divide figs among individual plates or bowls. Snip an "x" in tops of figs and open them like flowers. Pour syrup over them and drizzle heavy cream in a thin circle atop the pool of syrup encircling figs. May be served at room temperature or chilled.

Jacques Mokrani

Restaurateur Jacques Mokrani attributes his culinary talents to his mother. "I still remember coming home from school at lunchtime famished," he says. "On my way up the stairs to our apartment in Algiers, I would be tantalized by the aromas of her fabulous cooking." Inspired by his mother's meals, he was determined to learn all he could about preparing good food. Today, two classic rules guide his own cooking: In the marketplace, he never settles for second best, purchasing only the freshest seasonal produce and quality meats. And, he always readies food and equipment before starting to cook. He believes that with everything in place a cook can be more creative and efficient.

His menus exemplify the cooking of southern and southwestern France. The Provence-inspired main course of Menu 1, shrimp in tomato and garlic sauce, is accompanied by green beans and a *salade macédoine*, which is a variation on the classic mixture of vegetables or fruits. This side dish can be served, French style, as an appetizer.

In Menu 2, the entrée is *tournedos* with sauce *forestière*, which is made with wild mushrooms, Burgundy wine, and heavy cream. A potato *galette* and baked spinach complete the menu.

For Menu 3, Jacques Mokrani presents sautéed chicken pieces and mushrooms in a cream sauce with brandy and sherry. With this, he serves a rice pilaf and a mixed green salad.

For this colorful Provençal dinner, serve each guest three jumbo shrimp with their tails intact for a more dramatic presentation. Arrange the green beans around the shrimp, or serve them in a separate dish. Curly greens form a base for avocado, tomato, and onion salad.

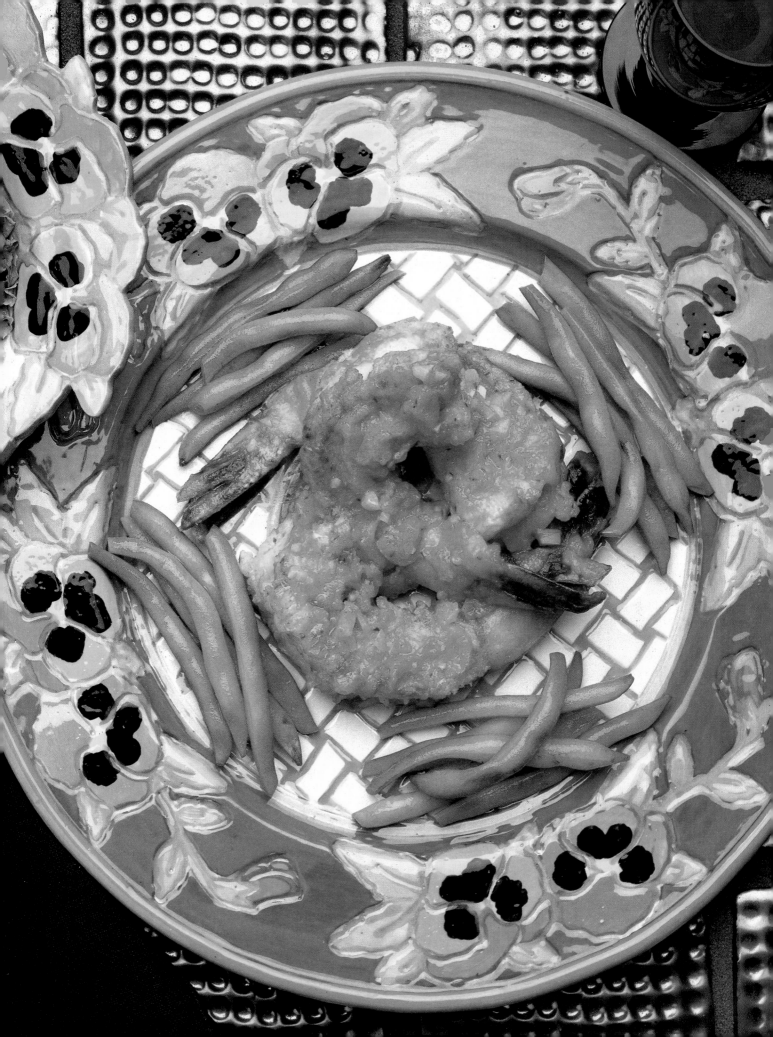

Shrimp Provençal
Haricots Verts
Salade Macédoine

Dip the jumbo shrimp in milk to tenderize them and then into flour, shaking off any excess. The milk-and-flour coating keeps the shrimp from sticking to the pan and gives them a beautiful golden brown color.

The sauce Provençal for the shrimp, redolent of garlic, is also seasoned with fresh thyme, an herb used frequently in Mediterranean dishes. Fresh thyme is sometimes hard to find in supermarkets or at greengrocers; however, dried thyme is an acceptable substitute.

The string beans are blanched, or plunged quickly into salted boiling water, which brings out their vivid green color and keeps them from overcooking. Blanching is a classic French technique that preserves the appearance and texture of many vegetables.

For the *salade macédoine*, use ripe avocados that are slightly soft to the touch and have no bruises or dark spots. An underripe avocado will mature quickly left in a paper bag at room temperature for a day or two.

WHAT TO DRINK

A crisp, fruity white wine tastes best with this menu. The first choice is a good California Sauvignon Blanc, but fine alternatives are a French Mâcon or Saint-Véran, or an Italian Sauvignon Blanc or Pinot Grigio.

SHOPPING LIST AND STAPLES

12 to 16 jumbo shrimp (about 1½ pounds
    total weight)
1 pound green beans
2 medium-size avocados, preferably the dark, knobby
    Hass variety
2 medium-size tomatoes
Small head escarole or curly endive
Small red or yellow onion
3 medium-size plus 1 small clove garlic
Small bunch parsley (optional)
1 lemon
½ cup milk
1 stick plus 2 tablespoons unsalted butter
Two 16-ounce cans Italian plum tomatoes
½ cup plus 1 teaspoon olive oil, or ⅓ cup olive oil plus
    3 tablespoons vegetable oil
2 tablespoons red wine vinegar
½ cup all-purpose flour, approximately
½ teaspoon dried thyme

Bay leaf
Salt and freshly ground pepper
¼ cup Cognac or other brandy

UTENSILS

Large skillet
Large saucepan
Large sauté pan
Medium-size sauté pan
2 pie plates
Large bowl
2 medium-size bowls, one heatproof
Colander
Strainer
Chef's knife
Paring knife
Wooden spoon
Metal tongs

START-TO-FINISH STEPS

1. Finely mince garlic for shrimp and sauce recipes.
2. Follow haricots recipe steps 1 through 3.
3. Follow salad recipe steps 1 through 4.
4. Follow haricots recipe steps 4 through 6.
5. Follow shrimp recipe steps 1 through 3.
6. Follow sauce recipe steps 1 through 3.
7. Follow shrimp recipe steps 4 through 9 and serve with haricots and salad.

RECIPES

Shrimp Provençal

12 to 16 jumbo shrimp (about 1½ pounds
    total weight)
½ cup milk
½ cup all-purpose flour, approximately
1 lemon
1 stick unsalted butter
¼ cup Cognac or other brandy
Small clove garlic, finely minced
Sauce Provençal (see following recipe)

1. Peel and devein shrimp, leaving tails intact. Place in colander, rinse under cold running water, and drain.
2. Pour milk into pie plate and flour into another pie plate.

With tongs, dip shrimp into milk and then into flour to coat thinly; shake off excess. Set aside on waxed paper.

3. Juice lemon and set aside.

4. In large skillet, melt 3 tablespoons butter over medium heat. When butter stops foaming, add shrimp and cook 2 minutes. Turn and cook another 2 minutes, or until golden.

5. While shrimp are cooking, place 4 dinner plates in 200-degree oven to warm.

6. Spoon off excess butter from pan. Remove pan from heat and add Cognac or other brandy. Return pan to medium heat and cook, stirring, 1 minute.

7. Add garlic and Sauce Provençal, and stir gently to combine.

8. Add remaining 5 tablespoons butter and lemon juice, and stir until butter is melted and incorporated, about 2 to 3 minutes.

9. Divide shrimp among warm dinner plates and serve immediately.

Sauce Provençal

Two 16-ounce cans Italian plum tomatoes
3 tablespoons olive or vegetable oil
3 medium-size cloves garlic, finely minced
½ teaspoon dried thyme
Bay leaf

1. Drain tomatoes in strainer set over medium-size bowl. Reserve liquid for another use. Chop tomatoes.

2. In large sauté pan, heat oil over medium-high heat until very hot and surface begins to shimmer. Add tomatoes and sauté briefly, about 1 minute.

3. Add garlic, thyme, and bay leaf, and cook, stirring, until tomatoes are reduced and thickened, about 3 minutes. Discard bay leaf. Set sauce aside.

Haricots Verts

Salt
1 pound green beans
2 tablespoons unsalted butter
Freshly ground pepper

1. Preheat oven to 200 degrees.

2. In large saucepan, bring 2 quarts of water and 2 teaspoons salt to a boil over medium-high heat.

3. Cut off stem ends of beans and remove strings.

4. Add beans to saucepan and let water return to a boil. Blanch 1 to 2 minutes.

5. Transfer beans to colander, refresh under cold running water, and drain. Set aside.

6. In medium-size sauté pan, melt butter over medium heat. Add beans and season with salt and pepper to taste. Sauté, tossing gently, 1 minute. Turn into heatproof bowl and keep warm in oven until ready to serve.

Salade Macédoine

2 medium-size tomatoes
Small red or yellow onion

2 medium-size avocados, preferably the dark, knobby Hass variety
2 tablespoons red wine vinegar
⅓ cup olive oil
Salt and freshly ground pepper
8 leaves escarole or curly endive
Small bunch parsley for garnish (optional)

1. Wash tomatoes and pat dry. Core and cut into wedges. Peel and finely chop enough onion to measure ½ cup. Peel, pit, and cut avocados into ¾-inch cubes.

2. Combine vegetables in large bowl. Add vinegar, olive oil, and salt and pepper to taste, and toss gently until vegetables are evenly coated with oil.

3. Wash escarole or endive and parsley, if using; pat dry with paper towels. Chop enough parsley to measure 2 tablespoons; set aside.

4. Arrange escarole or endive leaves in individual salad bowls. Top with vegetables and sprinkle with parsley, if desired. Cover and refrigerate until ready to serve.

ADDED TOUCH

Be sure to allow the caramel to harden completely before adding the crème. As the dessert bakes, the caramel will melt and become a rich sauce. Bake in a soufflé dish placed in a pan of water; this allows the crème to cook slowly and prevents it from either curdling or separating. Covering the crème caramel with foil while baking prevents a "skin" from forming on the surface.

Crème Caramel

1 cup sugar
1¼ cups milk
¼ cup heavy cream
2 teaspoons vanilla extract
2 whole eggs
1 egg yolk

1. In small saucepan, combine ¾ cup sugar with ¼ cup water and cook over high heat, without stirring, until golden brown in color. Immediately pour caramel into small soufflé dish and let harden completely, preferably overnight.

2. Preheat oven to 325 degrees.

3. In medium-size saucepan, bring milk and cream just to boiling point. Immediately set aside to cool until tepid.

4. In medium-size mixing bowl, combine remaining sugar, vanilla, whole eggs, and egg yolk.

5. Add cooled milk and cream to egg mixture and stir until blended.

6. Strain mixture into caramel-coated soufflé dish. Set soufflé dish in a larger pan and add enough water to reach halfway up side of dish. Top dish with a sheet of aluminum foil but do not crimp around edge. Bake 1¾ to 2 hours, or until a knife inserted in center comes out clean.

7. To serve, run a knife around the inside edge of dish to loosen custard. Turn out onto a platter, and serve warm or at room temperature.

Tournedos Forestière
Potato Galette
Baked Spinach

Good red wine complements the tournedos, *baked spinach, and potato* galette—*an elegant company meal.*

Grated potatoes, seasoned with chopped shallot, nutmeg, and ground pepper, are pressed into a skillet to form the *galette*, or round potato cake. To prevent the potatoes from discoloring, peel and grate them just before cooking. If you must prepare the potatoes ahead of time, put the shreds into a bowl of cold water and then, before cooking, squeeze them dry in paper towels to remove any excess moisture.

Tournedos are small steaks, one to two inches thick, cut from the eye of the beef tenderloin, close to the tip. These steaks are very tender and require only quick sautéing.

WHAT TO DRINK

Select a good red wine for this menu. An appropriate choice here would be a bottle from a Burgundian village such as Nuits-Saint-Georges, Fixin, or Morey-Saint-Denis.

SHOPPING LIST AND STAPLES

Four 4½-to 5-ounce tournedos (eye of beef tenderloin), 1 to 2 inches thick, trimmed and tied
½ pound fresh mushrooms
1½ pounds russet or large new potatoes
Small onion
Small shallot
Small bunch parsley (optional)
2 eggs
1 stick plus 2 tablespoons unsalted butter, approximately
1 pint heavy cream
Two 10-ounce packages frozen chopped spinach
2 tablespoons vegetable oil
Whole nutmeg, or 1 pinch of ground
Salt and freshly ground pepper
½ cup red Burgundy wine

UTENSILS

Food processor or grater
2 large skillets
Medium-size skillet with cover
Large sauté pan
Medium-size heavy-gauge saucepan
Large flat ovenproof plate
Medium-size soufflé dish or heatproof baking dish
Large bowl

2 medium-size bowls
Strainer
Measuring cups and spoons
Chef's knife
Paring knife
2 large metal spatulas
Rubber spatula
Wooden spoon
Balloon whisk
Vegetable peeler (optional)
Nutmeg grater (optional)

START-TO-FINISH STEPS

1. Grate whole nutmeg, if using, for potatoes and for spinach. Follow spinach recipe steps 1 through 6.
2. Follow potato recipe steps 1 through 4.
3. While potatoes are cooking, follow sauce recipe steps 1 through 3.
4. Turn potatoes and continue with sauce recipe step 4.
5. Follow spinach recipe step 7 and potato recipe step 5.
6. Follow tournedos recipe steps 1 through 5 and sauce recipe step 5.
7. Follow tournedos recipe step 6 and serve with potatoes and spinach.

RECIPES

Tournedos Forestière

2 tablespoons vegetable oil
Four 4½-to 5-ounce tournedos (eye of beef tenderloin), 1 to 2 inches thick, trimmed and tied
Salt
Small bunch parsley for garnish (optional)
Sauce Forestière (see following recipe)

1. In large skillet, heat oil over high heat until hot but not smoking.
2. While oil is heating, season tournedos on both sides with salt.
3. Place tournedos in skillet and cook each side 3 minutes for rare, 4 to 5 minutes for medium or medium-well, and 6 minutes for well done.
4. While meat is cooking, place dinner plates in 200-degree oven to warm.
5. Wash parsley, if using, and pat dry. Finely chop enough parsley to measure 1 tablespoon.

6. Using metal spatula, transfer tournedos to warm dinner plates and remove string. Top each with a few spoonfuls of Sauce Forestière and serve garnished with parsley, if desired.

Sauce Forestière

½ pound fresh mushrooms
3 tablespoons unsalted butter
Salt and freshly ground pepper
½ cup dry red Burgundy wine
½ cup heavy cream

1. Wipe mushrooms clean with damp paper towels. Thinly slice enough mushrooms to measure 2½ cups; set aside.
2. In large skillet, melt butter over medium-high heat. When butter stops foaming, add mushrooms, season with salt and pepper to taste, and sauté, stirring constantly, 4 minutes.
3. Increase heat to high. Add wine and cook, stirring constantly, until liquid is almost evaporated, about 8 minutes.
4. Add heavy cream and cook, stirring, until sauce thickens, about 2 to 3 minutes. Set aside.
5. Reheat sauce over medium heat, stirring occasionally, about 3 minutes.

Potato Galette

Small shallot
1½ pounds russet or large new potatoes
Pinch of nutmeg, preferably freshly grated
Salt and freshly ground pepper
5 tablespoons unsalted butter

1. Peel and finely chop shallot.
2. Fill medium-size bowl two thirds full with cold water. Peel potatoes, dropping each potato into the cold water as you finish peeling it. One by one, pat potatoes dry with paper towels and grate in food processor or with coarse side of grater. Rinse and dry bowl.
3. Combine shallot, potatoes, nutmeg, and salt and pepper to taste in medium-size bowl.
4. In medium-size skillet, melt butter over medium-high heat until sizzling. Add potatoes, pressing them down with back of spoon to make an even round layer. Cover, reduce heat to medium, and cook potatoes 10 minutes. Using 2 large metal spatulas, carefully turn potato cake, pressing down firmly again, and cook another 10 minutes.
5. With 2 spatulas, transfer *galette*, or cake, to large flat ovenproof plate and cut into 8 wedges. Keep warm in oven until ready to serve.

Baked Spinach

Salt
Two 10-ounce packages frozen chopped spinach
Small onion
2 tablespoons unsalted butter, approximately
Pinch of nutmeg, preferably freshly grated
Freshly ground pepper

2 eggs
⅓ cup heavy cream

1. Preheat oven to 325 degrees. Butter medium-size soufflé dish or heatproof baking dish.
2. In medium-size heavy-gauge saucepan, bring 2 cups water and 1 teaspoon salt to a boil over medium heat. Add spinach, cover, and simmer 5 minutes.
3. While spinach is simmering, peel and finely chop enough onion to measure 1 tablespoon.
4. Transfer spinach to strainer set over medium-size bowl and press with back of spoon to remove excess moisture. Rinse and dry bowl.
5. In large sauté pan, melt butter over medium-high heat. Add spinach, onion, nutmeg, and salt and pepper to taste. Sauté 3 to 4 minutes, adding more butter if necessary to prevent sticking, or until spinach is heated through. Remove pan from heat.
6. In medium-size bowl, whisk eggs with heavy cream until blended. Add to spinach mixture and stir to combine well. Turn into prepared soufflé dish and bake 25 minutes, or until lightly browned on top.
7. Remove dish from oven, cover loosely with foil, and keep warm on stove top until ready to serve. Reduce oven temperature to 200 degrees.

ADDED TOUCH

In this hot or cold side dish, which takes advantage of garden vegetables, black olives are a characteristic Niçoise touch.

Ratatouille Niçoise

3 tablespoons olive oil
Large onion, peeled and cut into ½-inch dice
Large green bell pepper, cored, halved, seeded, and cut into 1-inch x ½-inch pieces
4 small cloves garlic, peeled and coarsely chopped
Two 16-ounce cans Italian plum tomatoes, drained and diced
1 eggplant, peeled and cut into ½-inch cubes
2 medium-size zucchini, quartered lengthwise and cut into 1½-inch lengths
1 teaspoon dried thyme
Bay leaf
Salt and freshly ground pepper
10 pitted black olives, halved

1. In large saucepan, heat olive oil over medium heat. Add onion and bell pepper, and cook, covered, until just softened but not browned, 3 to 5 minutes.
2. Increase heat to medium-high, stir in garlic and tomatoes, and cook 6 to 7 minutes.
3. Add diced eggplant, zucchini, thyme, bay leaf, and salt and pepper to taste. Stir in olives and cook, covered, about 10 minutes, or until eggplant is softened. Be careful not to overcook or the vegetables will disintegrate. Ratatouille should have more bulk than a purée.
4. Turn into a bowl and serve hot or cold, as desired.

Sautéed Chicken Basquaise
Rice Pilaf
Watercress and Belgian Endive Salad

The sautéed chicken in cream sauce flavored with sherry is accompanied by rice pilaf, mixed salad, and crusty French bread.

Fresh mushrooms enhance the flavor of the thick wine sauce for this chicken entrée. Shiitake mushrooms, with their velvety brown caps and pronounced aroma are recommended. They are available fresh or dried from Oriental groceries and well-stocked supermarkets. If you cannot find shiitakes, as an alternative, use fresh or dried chanterelles, which are more authentically French. You may find fresh chanterelles (trumpet-shaped and golden in color) at quality greengrocers. Often they are very gritty and should be rinsed quickly under cold running water. Never subject mushrooms to soaking; it destroys their delicate flavor.

WHAT TO DRINK

A medium-bodied dry white wine is called for here. Try a simple French Chablis or Sancerre, or choose a dry California Chenin Blanc or Riesling.

SHOPPING LIST AND STAPLES

1 frying chicken, cut into 8 pieces, or 8 chicken thighs (about 2¼ pounds total weight)
½ pound fresh shiitake or chanterelle mushrooms, or 4 ounces dried chanterelles

2 small heads Belgian endive
1 red bell pepper (optional)
2 bunches watercress
Small bunch scallions
2 medium-size shallots
Small bunch parsley (optional)
1 lemon
1 egg
½ pint heavy cream
6 tablespoons unsalted butter
2¼ cups chicken stock, preferably homemade
   (see page 11), or canned
½ cup olive oil
1 teaspoon white wine vinegar
1 cup converted long-grain rice
½ teaspoon sugar
2 to 3 whole cloves
Salt
Freshly ground black pepper
Freshly ground white pepper
¼ cup brandy or Cognac
½ cup dry sherry

UTENSILS

Large cast-iron skillet with cover
Medium-size heavy-gauge saucepan with cover
Large salad bowl
Large bowl
2 small bowls, plus one additional if using dried
   mushrooms
Colander
Salad spinner (optional)
Measuring cups and spoons
Chef's knife
Paring knife
Wooden spoon
Juicer (optional)
Small whisk
Tongs

START-TO-FINISH STEPS

Thirty minutes ahead: If using dried mushrooms, place
them in a small bowl and add warm water to cover.

1. Follow rice pilaf recipe steps 1 through 4.
2. Follow salad recipes steps 1 through 3.

3. Follow chicken recipe steps 1 through 4.
4. Turn off heat under rice, step 5, and follow chicken
recipe steps 5 and 6.
5. While sauce is reducing, follow salad recipe steps 4 and 5.
6. Follow chicken recipe step 7 and salad recipe step 6.
7. Follow chicken recipe step 8 and serve with rice and
salad.

RECIPES

Sautéed Chicken Basquaise

4 tablespoons unsalted butter
1 frying chicken, cut into 8 pieces, or 8 chicken thighs
   (about 2¼ pounds total weight)
Salt
Freshly ground black pepper
2 medium-size shallots
½ pound fresh shiitake or chanterelle mushrooms, or
   4 ounces dried chanterelles, reconstituted
1 red bell pepper for garnish (optional)
Small bunch parsley for garnish (optional)
¼ cup brandy or Cognac
½ cup dry sherry
⅔ cup heavy cream

1. In large heavy-gauge skillet, melt butter over medium-
high heat.
2. While butter is melting, season chicken pieces with salt
and pepper to taste.
3. Add chicken pieces to skillet and cook on one side 4 to 5
minutes, or until brown. Using tongs, turn chicken and
cook another 4 to 5 minutes.
4. While chicken is browning, peel and chop enough shallots to measure 3 tablespoons. If using fresh mushrooms,
rinse under cold water, pat dry with paper towels, and cut
in half. If using reconstituted dried mushrooms, rinse
under cold running water and pat dry with paper towels;
cut in half. If using red bell pepper or parsley for garnish,
wash and pat dry. Core, halve, and seed pepper. Cut into
⅛-inch-wide strips. Trim parsley and chop enough to measure 1 tablespoon. Set aside.
5. When chicken has browned, spoon off fat. Remove skillet from heat and add brandy or Cognac. Return skillet to
low heat and, using wooden spoon, scrape up any brown
bits clinging to pan, stirring to combine with liquid. Continue cooking until brandy is almost evaporated.
6. Add shallots and mushrooms to skillet, and stir gently

to combine. Add sherry and continue cooking over low heat, stirring, until liquid is reduced by half, about 7 minutes.

7. Stir in cream and simmer until sauce is thick enough to coat a wooden spoon, about 5 minutes.

8. Divide chicken pieces among individual dinner plates, top with mushroom sauce, and serve garnished with parsley or topped with red pepper strips, if desired.

Rice Pilaf

Small bunch scallions
2 tablespoons unsalted butter
2¼ cups chicken stock, preferably homemade (see page 11), or canned
2 to 3 whole cloves
1 cup converted long-grain rice

1. Chop enough scallions to measure 2 tablespoons.
2. In medium-size heavy-gauge saucepan, melt butter over low heat. Add scallions and sauté until wilted, about 2 minutes.
3. Add stock and 2 to 3 cloves, according to taste, increase heat to high, and bring to a rolling boil.
4. Stir in rice and return mixture to a boil. Cover, reduce heat to very low, and simmer until the rice has absorbed all the stock, about 18 minutes.
5. Turn off heat and keep covered until ready to serve.

Watercress and Belgian Endive Salad

1 lemon
2 bunches watercress
2 small heads Belgian endive
1 egg
½ teaspoon sugar
¼ teaspoon salt
Freshly ground white pepper
1 teaspoon white wine vinegar
½ cup olive oil

1. Squeeze enough lemon to measure 2 tablespoons juice.
2. Immerse watercress in large bowl of cold water and agitate to dislodge any grit. Trim off stems and discard. Drain watercress in colander and dry in salad spinner or pat dry with paper towels. Place in large salad bowl.
3. Wash endive and slice into ½-inch-thick rounds; add to watercress in salad bowl. Cover bowl with plastic wrap and refrigerate until ready to serve.

4. Using two small bowls, separate egg white and yolk, reserving white for another use. Add lemon juice, salt, and pepper to taste, and whisk until salt is dissolved. Add vinegar and whisk briskly until bubbles appear on surface.
5. In a slow, steady stream, add olive oil to mixture, whisking continuously until dressing acquires a creamy texture. Refrigerate until ready to serve.
6. Just before serving, pour dressing over salad and toss gently. Divide among individual plates.

ADDED TOUCH

When washing beaters, be sure to remove any trace of yolk before beating the whites or you will not achieve the volume necessary for this chilled soufflé.

Iced Lemon Soufflé

2 medium-size lemons
½ cup heavy cream
1 teaspoon vanilla extract
5 eggs
½ cup sugar
Pinch of salt
1 envelope unflavored gelatin

1. Juice 1 lemon and set aside. Grate enough of remaining lemon to measure 1 tablespoon zest, being careful to avoid white pith.
2. Lightly grease inside of medium-size soufflé dish with vegetable oil or butter. Tie a waxed-paper collar around top of soufflé dish.
3. In bowl of electric mixer, whip heavy cream with vanilla until stiff. Turn into medium-size bowl.
4. Separate eggs, sliding yolks into a small bowl and whites into a large bowl. Add sugar to yolks and beat at high speed 10 minutes, or until mixture becomes very thick.
5. Wash beaters thoroughly and whip egg whites with salt until they form stiff peaks.
6. Using rubber spatula, gently fold whipped cream into egg whites. Add thickened egg yolk mixture and lemon zest, and fold just until incorporated.
7. In small saucepan, combine lemon juice with gelatin. Warm slightly over low heat until gelatin dissolves. When cool, gently stir gelatin into soufflé mixture.
8. Turn mixture into soufflé dish and refrigerate at least 2 hours before serving.

John Case

F rench regional recipes, with their emphasis on fresh indigenous produce, suit John Case's style of cooking: "I try to preserve the character and integrity of each ingredient, and I use local seasonal foods when I cook," he says. For him, this means no elaborate sauces or multiplicity of ingredients.

For his three menus, he selects dishes representative of Provence, Lyons, and Périgord, respectively. The black bass main dish of Menu 1 is reminiscent of a Provençal specialty, sea bass grilled with fennel stalks. Here black bass fillets and sliced fennel stalks are covered with Romaine leaves and baked. Saffron colors and flavors the accompanying rice.

Menu 2 highlights foods that are associated with the city of Lyons: poultry, here prepared as stuffed chicken breasts, and potatoes, which the cook shreds and forms into a pie. John Case's third menu features omelets filled with mushrooms, a Périgourdine specialty. The stuffed vegetables contain a variety of herbs, cheeses, and nuts.

Black bass fillets, flavored with sliced fennel, are covered with Romaine leaves to make an appetizing entrée for an informal dinner. Golden saffron rice accompanies the fish. For the salad, arrange tomato slices and coarsely grated celery root decoratively on side plates, and garnish with a stem of arugula.

Tomato and Celery Root Salad with Chèvre Dressing
Black Bass with Fennel and Romaine
Saffron Rice

Crisp slices of fennel bake with the black bass and impart a slight anise flavor. Florence fennel, or *finocchio*, has a flattened bulbous base and long green stalks. Select firm bulbs without brown spots. Fennel is usually available from September through April, with December being its peak month. If you cannot find it, use the same amount of sliced celery plus ½ teaspoon fennel seed, or aniseed, for a similar flavor.

WHAT TO DRINK

A crisp dry white wine would counter the richness of this menu. Try a California Sauvignon Blanc, a Pouilly-Fumé, or a white Bordeaux, such as Entre-Deux-Mers.

SHOPPING LIST AND STAPLES

Four 6- to 8-ounce black bass fillets, each about ½ inch thick
Large fennel bulb (about 1 pound)
Large celery root (about ¾ pound)
Small onion
1 head Romaine
Small bunch arugula or watercress
4 medium-size tomatoes (about 1¼ pounds total weight)
Small bunch fresh basil, or 1 teaspoon dried
2 medium-size cloves plus 1 large clove garlic
1 stick plus 1 tablespoon unsalted butter
¼ pound mild chèvre, preferably Montrachet, or feta cheese
2½ cups chicken stock, preferably homemade (see page 11), or canned
¾ cup olive oil or light vegetable oil
¼ cup balsamic, red wine, or tarragon vinegar
1 cup long-grain white rice
1 teaspoon saffron threads (about ½ ounce)
Salt
⅓ cup dry white wine

UTENSILS

Food processor or blender
Large skillet
Medium-size saucepan
2 small saucepans, one with tight-fitting cover
13 x 9 x 2-inch baking dish
Colander
Measuring cups and spoons
Chef's knife
Paring knife
Wooden spoon
Grater
Vegetable peeler (optional)
Pastry brush

START-TO-FINISH STEPS

1. Follow rice recipe steps 1 and 2.
2. While onion is wilting, follow bass recipe step 1.
3. Follow rice recipe steps 3 through 5.
4. Follow bass recipe steps 2 through 5.
5. Follow salad recipe steps 1 and 2, and rice recipe step 6.
6. Follow bass recipe step 6 and salad recipe steps 3 and 4.
7. Follow bass recipe step 7, rice recipe step 7, and serve with salad.

RECIPES

Tomato and Celery Root Salad with Chèvre Dressing

Large clove garlic
Small bunch arugula or watercress
2 to 3 large leaves fresh basil, or 1 teaspoon dried
¼ pound mild chèvre, preferably Montrachet, or feta cheese
¼ cup balsamic, red wine, or tarragon vinegar
¾ cup olive oil or light vegetable oil
4 medium-size tomatoes (about 1¼ pounds)
Large celery root (about ¾ pound total weight)

1. Peel garlic and cut in half. Wash arugula or watercress and fresh basil, if using, and pat dry with paper towels. Trim off stem ends. Cut chèvre into small chunks.
2. In food processor or blender, combine garlic, basil, chèvre, vinegar, and oil, and purée until smooth, about 1 minute. Leave dressing in processor.
3. Wash, core, and cut each tomato crosswise into 4 slices. Peel celery root and grate coarsely, or cut into ⅛-inch julienne strips. Divide tomato slices equally among 4 salad plates. Mound celery root beside tomatoes and garnish each serving with a stem of arugula.
4. Just before serving, process dressing to recombine and spoon over each salad.

Black Bass with Fennel and Romaine

Large fennel bulb (about 1 pound)
Four 6- to 8-ounce black bass fillets, each about
  ½ inch thick
2 medium-size cloves garlic
⅓ cup dry white wine
1 stick unsalted butter
6 to 8 leaves Romaine

1. Preheat oven to 350 degrees. Cut off bulbous base of fennel. Separate stalks, wash in cold water, and pat dry. Select 8 to 10 stalks and reserve remainder for another use (see LEFTOVER SUGGESTION). Cut each stalk in half crosswise. Peel and mince garlic.
2. In large skillet, bring ½ inch of water to a boil. Add fennel, cover, and simmer until crisp-tender, about 10 minutes.
3. While fennel is simmering, melt 4 tablespoons butter in small saucepan over low heat.
4. Rinse bass fillets under cold running water and pat dry with paper towels. Generously grease shallow baking dish. Place fish in dish and sprinkle each fillet with one quarter of the minced garlic. Pour wine over fish and dot each fillet with 1 tablespoon butter, cut into small pieces, and top with 4 slices of fennel. Brush with half of melted butter.
5. Bake fish 10 to 15 minutes, depending on thickness of fillets, just until firm but undercooked.
6. Wash Romaine leaves and dry in salad spinner or pat dry with paper towels. Drape Romaine leaves loosely over fish, and brush with remaining melted butter. Bake another 5 minutes, or until fish is still firm but flaky.
7. Divide fillets among dinner plates.

Saffron Rice

Small onion
1 tablespoon unsalted butter
1 teaspoon saffron threads (about ½ ounce)
1 cup long-grain white rice
2½ cups chicken stock, preferably homemade
  (see page 11), or canned
1 teaspoon salt

1. Peel and chop enough onion to measure about ½ cup.
2. In medium-size saucepan, melt butter over medium heat. Add onion and sauté 3 to 5 minutes, or until soft and translucent.
3. Stir in saffron threads and sauté about 1 minute.
4. Add rice and cook, stirring, about 3 minutes, or until rice is evenly colored, heated through, and translucent.
5. While rice is cooking, bring chicken stock to a boil in small saucepan over high heat. Pour stock over rice, add salt, and cover. Reduce heat to low and simmer rice gently 15 to 20 minutes, or until stock is just absorbed.
6. Turn off heat and allow rice to stand, covered, until ready to serve.
7. Fluff rice with fork and divide among dinner plates.

█████████
ADDED TOUCH

Instead of a raspberry-cream filling for this delicate, airy cake, you can use any kind of berries in season, diced peaches, or sliced bananas.

Walnut Meringue Torte

1 cup walnuts
6 large eggs
½ teaspoon salt
1¾ cups plus 4 teaspoons sugar
½ teaspoon vanilla extract
¼ teaspoon apple cider vinegar
1½ cups heavy cream
½ pint raspberries, washed and hulled
Confectioners' sugar for garnish

1. Preheat oven to 350 degrees.
2. Arrange walnuts in a single layer in baking pan. Toast in oven, shaking pan occasionally to prevent scorching, 12 minutes or until golden brown. Remove from oven and allow to cool. Raise oven temperature to 375 degrees.
3. For meringue, separate eggs, reserving yolks for another use. Combine egg whites and salt in medium-size bowl. Using electric mixer, beat until foamy. While still beating, gradually add 1½ cups sugar and beat until stiff peaks form.
4. In food processor or with nut grinder, grind walnuts. Add nuts, vanilla, and vinegar to egg whites, and beat with electric mixer on slow speed until blended.
5. Butter two 8-inch round cake pans and then line with buttered waxed paper. Sprinkle with flour and tilt pans to coat evenly.
6. Divide batter between pans and bake 30 to 40 minutes, or until meringue pulls away from sides of pans. Wash mixing bowl and beaters, dry, and put in refrigerator to chill.
7. Cool meringues in pans for 10 minutes and turn out onto rack. Remove waxed paper and cool completely.
8. In chilled bowl, whip heavy cream with chilled beaters until stiff peaks form.
9. For torte base, spread one meringue with two thirds of the whipped cream and sprinkle with remaining ¼ cup plus 4 teaspoons sugar. Reserving 8 raspberries for top, spread raspberries over cream.
10. Top filling with second meringue. Spread half of remaining whipped cream over top meringue layer.
11. Fit pastry bag with star tip, fill with remaining whipped cream, and pipe 8 rosettes on top layer. Place a raspberry in each rosette, and lightly dust entire top of torte with confectioners' sugar.

█████████
LEFTOVER SUGGESTION

Mince extra fennel leaves finely and use them as a garnish for soups, salads, and vegetable dishes. Trim any remaining fennel stalks to serve with cheese dips, or slice them into a tossed salad.

Lettuce Salad with Orange-Lemon Dressing
Ballotines of Chicken
Shredded Potato Pie

For an impressive buffet, serve rolled and stuffed chicken breasts with shredded potatoes that have been baked in an attractive pie dish—or unmold the potatoes if you prefer. Offer the salad on a decorative platter.

B*allotine* is a French culinary term describing boned meat, fowl, or fish that is stuffed, rolled, and then skewered into a "bundle" shape for cooking. Here, John Case uses boneless chicken breasts with the skins on and makes a filling of chicken livers, mushrooms, and onions.

WHAT TO DRINK

For this menu, the cook suggests a white Burgundy, such as a Mâcon. You could also try a Beaujolais.

SHOPPING LIST AND STAPLES

4 boneless chicken breasts, with skin attached (each about ½ pound)
½ pound chicken livers
½ pound mushrooms
Medium-size red onion
2 small plus 1 large yellow onion
3 large potatoes (about 1½ pounds total weight)
2 heads Bibb or 1 head Boston lettuce
Small bunch parsley
2 small cloves garlic
3 oranges
1 lemon
4 eggs
1 cup milk
7 tablespoons unsalted butter
2 ounces Parmesan cheese
⅓ cup olive oil
2 tablespoons red wine vinegar
1 tablespoon Dijon mustard
1 tablespoon flour
1 teaspoon ground allspice
Salt
Freshly ground black and white pepper
½ cup dry red wine, or white wine, if preferred

UTENSILS

Food processor or blender
Medium-size heavy skillet
Medium-size saucepan
14 x 10-inch roasting pan
9-inch ovenproof pie dish
Medium-size bowl
2 small bowls

Colander
Medium-size sieve
Salad spinner (optional)
Measuring cups and spoons
Chef's knife
Paring knife
Wooden spoon
Whisk
Vegetable peeler (optional)
Grater (if not using food processor)
Juicer
Mallet or rolling pin
Large wooden toothpicks or small skewers

START-TO-FINISH STEPS

1. Follow potato recipe steps 1 through 3.
2. Follow chicken recipe steps 1 through 5.
3. Follow salad recipe steps 1 through 4.
4. Follow chicken recipe step 6 and salad recipe step 5.
5. Follow chicken recipe step 7 and serve with salad and potato pie.

RECIPES

Lettuce Salad with Orange-Lemon Dressing

2 heads Bibb or 1 head Boston lettuce
Medium-size red onion
2 small cloves garlic
3 oranges
1 lemon
1 egg
1 tablespoon Dijon mustard
1 tablespoon red wine vinegar
⅓ cup olive oil
Salt and freshly ground black pepper

1. Wash lettuce leaves and dry in salad spinner or pat dry with paper towels. Peel onion. In food processor fitted with slicing disk or with chef's knife, cut onion into paper-thin slices. Peel and chop garlic.
2. Arrange lettuce leaves on platter, or on 4 individual plates, if preferred, and top with half the onion rings.
3. With paring knife, peel 2 oranges, removing as much white pith as possible. Segment oranges by cutting along both sides of membranes, or cut crosswise into ¼-inch-thick slices. Arrange oranges over onion and lettuce and top with remaining onion rings. Cover and refrigerate until ready to serve.
4. Juice remaining orange and lemon. In small bowl, combine the fruit juices, egg, and mustard. Add garlic and remaining ingredients, and whisk until blended.
5. Just before serving, whisk dressing to recombine and spoon over salad.

Ballotines of Chicken

½ pound chicken livers
½ pound mushrooms

4 tablespoons unsalted butter
Small yellow onion, peeled and chopped
4 sprigs parsley, chopped
1 teaspoon ground allspice
4 boneless chicken breasts, with skin attached
    (each about ½ pound)
Salt and freshly ground black pepper
1 tablespoon flour
½ cup dry red wine, or white wine, if preferred

1. Preheat oven to 450 degrees. Rinse chicken livers, pat dry with paper towels, and remove membranes and fat. Wipe mushrooms clean with damp paper towels and chop.
2. In medium-size skillet, melt 2 tablespoons butter over medium heat. Add chicken livers, mushrooms, onion, parsley, and allspice, and sauté, stirring continuously, 5 to 7 minutes, or until livers are no longer pink.
3. Transfer sautéed chicken livers to food processor or blender and purée until smooth; set aside.
4. Place each chicken breast between 2 sheets of waxed paper and pound with mallet or rolling pin to ¼-inch thickness. Place each breast skin side down and season with salt and pepper. Mound one fourth of liver mixture in center of each breast. Fold sides of breast over filling and secure with toothpicks or small skewers.
5. Place ballotines in medium-size roasting pan skin side up and dot each with about ½ tablespoon butter. Bake until skin is brown, juices run clear, and meat is tender when pierced with a skewer, 20 to 25 minutes.
6. Transfer ballotines to serving platter, remove toothpicks, and cover loosely with foil to keep warm.
7. Pour off all but 1 tablespoon fat from roasting pan. Stir in flour and cook over medium heat, stirring, 1 minute. Add red or white wine to deglaze pan, scraping up any bits of chicken from bottom of pan. Strain sauce through sieve set over small bowl. Pour sauce over chicken and serve.

Shredded Potato Pie

Large yellow onion
3 large potatoes (about 1½ pounds total weight)
3 tablespoons unsalted butter
1 cup milk
3 eggs, lightly beaten
½ cup freshly grated Parmesan cheese
Salt and freshly ground white pepper

1. Peel onion and potatoes. In food processor fitted with shredding disk or with coarse side of grater, shred onion and potatoes. In colander, rinse shredded vegetables under cold water, drain well, pressing with back of spoon to remove water, and pat dry with paper towels.
2. In medium-size saucepan, combine butter and milk, and heat over medium heat just until butter melts. Stir in shredded potato-onion mixture, eggs, Parmesan, and salt and pepper to taste, and cook, tossing until mixture is combined and heated through.
3. Generously butter a 9-inch ovenproof pie dish. Turn mixture into dish, and bake, uncovered, in 450-degree oven 45 minutes, or until crisp and lightly browned.

Wild Mushroom Omelets
Stuffed Vegetables

For a family supper or Sunday brunch, offer each guest a mushroom-filled omelet and a selection of stuffed vegetables.

Before you make the omelets, have the rest of the menu prepared and your guests seated. You will be able to cook and serve four omelets in less than fifteen minutes. For a puffier omelet, bring the eggs to room temperature. Use a non-stick or well-seasoned pan to keep the eggs from sticking, and make sure it is hot before you add the butter and the eggs. It is the right temperature when a drop of water skitters on the surface.

WHAT TO DRINK

For a festive touch, the cook suggests you serve a sparkling wine. Choose one from Touraine or the Loire Valley, or try a California Brut.

SHOPPING LIST AND STAPLES

½ pound shiitakes, chanterelles, cèpes, oyster, or other fresh mushrooms
8 to 12 extra-large mushrooms with 2-inch wide caps
2 baby eggplants
4 medium-size tomatoes (about ¾ pound total weight)
Large shallot
1 clove garlic
Small bunch fresh basil, or ½ teaspoon dried
1 dozen large eggs
6 tablespoons unsalted butter
2 ounces cream cheese
2 ounces Parmesan cheese

3 tablespoons vegetable oil
1 teaspoon Worcestershire sauce
3½-ounce jar capers
½ cup fresh bread crumbs
2-ounce jar pine nuts
Salt
Freshly ground black and white pepper
2 tablespoons dry white vermouth

UTENSILS

Food processor
Medium-size heavy-gauge skillet with cover
Small skillet
8-inch omelet pan
13 x 9 x 2-inch baking dish
2 medium-size bowls
Measuring cups and spoons
Chef's knife
Paring knife
Wooden spoon
Whisk
Grater (if not using food processor)

START-TO-FINISH STEPS

One hour ahead: Set out eggs for omelets. For vegetables recipe, set out cream cheese.

Ten minutes ahead: Clarify butter for omelets (see page 10).

1. Follow vegetables recipe steps 1 through 9.
2. Follow omelets recipe steps 1 through 9, vegetables recipe 10, and serve.

RECIPES

Wild Mushroom Omelets

½ pound shiitakes, chanterelles, cèpes, oyster, or other
    fresh mushrooms
Large shallot
6 tablespoons unsalted butter, clarified
2 tablespoons dry white vermouth
12 large eggs
Salt and freshly ground white pepper
1 teaspoon Worcestershire sauce

1. Wipe mushrooms clean with damp paper towels. Trim off stems, reserving for another use, and cut mushrooms into ⅛-inch-thick slices. Peel and mince shallot; set aside.
2. Place 4 dinner plates under hot running water to warm.
3. In medium-size skillet, heat 2 tablespoons clarified butter over medium heat. Add shallots and sauté 2 to 3 minutes, or until soft. Add three quarters of sliced mushrooms and sauté 3 to 5 minutes, or just until tender. Stir in dry vermouth. Remove from heat and cover to keep warm.
4. Whisk eggs with salt and white pepper to taste. Add Worcestershire and whisk until foamy.
5. Dry dinner plates.
6. Add 2 teaspoons clarified butter to omelet pan, tilting

pan so that sides are evenly coated, and place pan over medium heat. When pan is hot, add one quarter of egg mixture and allow to set, about ½ minute. With fork, gently pull cooked edges toward center of pan, tilting pan so uncooked egg runs to edges, about 3 minutes.
7. Place one quarter of sautéed mushrooms on portion of omelet near handle of pan. Tilt pan and, using fork, fold omelet over mushrooms toward handle. Then roll folded, filled omelet onto warm plate.
8. Repeat steps 6 and 7 three more times.
9. Garnish omelets with remaining sliced mushrooms.

Stuffed Vegetables

2 baby eggplants
4 medium-size tomatoes (about ¾ pound total weight)
8 to 12 extra-large mushrooms with 2-inch-wide caps
1 clove garlic
½ cup fresh bread crumbs
Salt and freshly ground black pepper
1 or 2 fresh basil leaves, or ½ teaspoon dried
3 tablespoons vegetable oil
2 ounces cream cheese, at room temperature
¼ cup freshly grated Parmesan cheese
1 tablespoon pine nuts
1 tablespoon capers, drained

1. Wash eggplants and tomatoes, and pat dry. Cut eggplants in half lengthwise and scoop out pulp, leaving ¼-inch shell. Reserve pulp. Cut ¼-inch-thick slice from tops of tomatoes and scoop out pulp. Reserve pulp. Wipe mushrooms clean with damp paper towels. Trim off stems. Dice stems, tops, and reserved pulp. Peel and mince garlic.
2. In medium-size bowl, combine diced vegetable mixture, garlic, bread crumbs, and salt and pepper to taste.
3. For tomatoes, wash fresh basil, if using, pat dry, and chop.
4. Preheat oven to 400 degrees.
5. In small skillet, heat 1 tablespoon oil over medium heat. Add one third of vegetable mixture and sauté 2 minutes.
6. For stuffing eggplants: Add cream cheese to sautéed vegetable mixture and stir until combined and heated through. Divide stuffing between eggplants. Wipe out pan with paper towels.
7. For stuffing tomatoes: Add 1 tablespoon oil to pan and return to medium heat. Add one third of vegetable mixture and sauté 2 minutes. Add basil and Parmesan, and stir until combined and heated through. Divide stuffing among tomatoes. Wipe out pan with paper towels.
8. Add 1 tablespoon oil to pan and return to medium heat. Add remainder of vegetable mixture and sauté 2 minutes. Add ½ tablespoon pine nuts and capers, and sauté 1 minute. Divide stuffing among mushrooms.
9. Place the stuffed vegetables in large shallow baking dish. Bake 15 to 20 minutes, or until stuffing is browned and vegetables are cooked through.
10. Cut eggplants in half crosswise. Divide vegetables among dinner plates and garnish mushrooms with remaining pine nuts.

Dennis Gilbert

MENU 1 (Right)
Tourte à la Périgourdine
Mixed Green Salad

MENU 2
Sautéed Chicken Breasts with
Vegetables and Summer Savory Butter
Aligot

MENU 3
Veal Scallops with Saffron Apples
Lentils with Tomatoes and Bacon
Sorrel and Celery Root Salad

Dennis Gilbert describes himself as a man who cooks for the love of it, acknowledging that his travels through northern Europe have been a major influence upon his food career, as were his experiences as a student and amateur cook at the University of Iowa. He has worked as a professional cook in a number of restaurants, and now is head chef at his own establishment. He believes that the presentation of a meal is very important, but that "dining is more than looking and smelling. People should have a substantial meal to sit down to."

For that reason, he has selected three menus from Périgord and the Auvergne, where sizable meals are commonplace. Menu 1 features *tourte à la périgourdine*, an adaptation of chicken pie that is ideal for a winter supper. *Tourte* comes from the Latin *tortus*, which means making round.

Menu 2, from the Auvergne, offers sautéed chicken breasts and *aligot*, a potato and cheese casserole. The word comes from *aligoter*, "to cut," and in a true *aligot* the melted cheese forms long ribbons that have to be cut when the dish is served.

Menu 3, also Auvergnac, consists of sautéed veal scallops with three distinctive side dishes: saffron apples, lentils with tomatoes and bacon, and a salad of celery root and sorrel. The lentil dish, according to Dennis Gilbert, orginated in the town of Le Puy.

The golden crust of the main-dish chicken pie is flecked with chopped parsley and decorated with pastry leaves. Garnish the mixed green salad with grated Parmesan and, if you wish, serve warm French bread as an accompaniment.

64

Tourte à la Périgourdine
Mixed Green Salad

For his version of this poultry pie, the cook uses fresh mushrooms and chicken livers in place of the truffles and *foie gras* of the traditional Périgord dish. Select chicken livers that are plump, moist, odor free, and dark red. Trim away any membrane and fat before cooking. Madeira, a fortified wine with a sediment, should be re-corked after opening and stored on its side.

WHAT TO DRINK

A medium-bodied red wine would best accompany this hearty menu. Good choices include a Saint-Émilion or a California Zinfandel or Merlot.

SHOPPING LIST AND STAPLES

1 pound skinless, boneless chicken breasts
½ pound chicken livers
½ pound mushrooms
Large head Boston lettuce
Large head red leaf lettuce
Medium-size tomato
2 to 3 large shallots
2 cloves garlic
1 bunch parsley
1 lemon
1 egg
1 stick plus 6 tablespoons unsalted butter
¼ pound lard
2 ounces Parmesan cheese
1½ cups chicken stock, preferably homemade
  (see page 11), or canned
¼ cup plus 2 tablespoons extra-virgin olive oil
2¼ cups all-purpose flour, approximately
¾ teaspoon fennel seed
¾ teaspoon dried marjoram
Salt and freshly ground pepper
¾ cup Madeira wine

UTENSILS

Large heavy-gauge skillet or sauté pan
Small saucepan
9-inch pie pan
Salad bowl
2 large bowls
2 small bowls

Strainer
Salad spinner (optional)
Measuring cups and spoons
Chef's knife
Paring knife
Large wooden spoon
Slotted spoon
Wooden spatula
Whisk
Grater
Pastry cutter (optional)
Rolling pin
Pastry brush

START-TO-FINISH STEPS

Thirty minutes ahead: For tourte recipe, chill 5 tablespoons butter and ⅓ cup lard in freezer; clarify 1 stick plus 1 tablespoon butter (see page 10) and set aside.

1. Follow tourte recipe steps 1 through 9.
2. Follow salad recipe step 1.
3. Follow tourte recipe step 10.
4. While tourte is baking, follow salad recipe steps 2 and 3.
5. Follow tourte recipe step 11 and salad recipe step 4.
6. Follow tourte recipe step 12 and serve with salad.

RECIPES
Tourte à la Périgourdine

Pastry:
1 bunch parsley
2¼ cups all-purpose flour, approximately
1 teaspoon salt
⅓ cup butter, well chilled
⅓ cup lard, well chilled

Filling:
1 pound skinless, boneless chicken breasts
½ pound chicken livers
½ pound mushrooms
2 to 3 large shallots
2 cloves garlic
Medium-size tomato
1 stick plus 1 tablespoon unsalted butter, clarified
3 tablespoons all-purpose flour
1½ cups chicken stock
¾ cup Madeira wine

¾ teaspoon dried marjoram
¾ teaspoon fennel seed
Salt and freshly ground black pepper
1 egg

1. Wash parsley and pat dry with paper towels. Chop enough to measure ½ cup; set aside.
2. In large mixing bowl, combine 2 cups flour and salt. Using pastry cutter, or two knives, cut in chilled butter and lard until mixture resembles coarse cornmeal. Stir in parsley. Sprinkle dough with about ¼ cup ice water, and mix gently with fork to form ball.
3. Grease 9-inch pie plate. On lightly floured surface, roll out two thirds of pastry into a circle large enough to line pie plate. Roll pastry loosely around pin and unroll over pie plate, gently fitting the pastry into the plate. Roughly trim edges and set in freezer to chill thoroughly. Roll out remaining dough to form top crust. Place between 2 sheets of waxed paper and refrigerate.
4. Cut chicken breasts into ½-inch cubes. Wash chicken livers and pat dry with paper towels. Remove membranes and trim off any excess fat. Wipe mushrooms clean with damp paper towels and cut into ¼-inch-thick slices. Peel and mince shallots and garlic. Wash tomato and pat dry. Peel, core, halve, seed, and chop tomato. Set prepared ingredients aside.
5. Preheat oven to 450 degrees. In large skillet, heat ¼ cup clarified butter over medium-high heat. Add chicken cubes, livers, and mushrooms, and sauté, stirring constantly, 5 minutes. With slotted spoon, transfer mixture to large bowl.
6. For sauce, add remaining clarified butter to skillet. Still over medium-high heat, add shallots and garlic, and sauté, stirring constantly, 3 minutes. Sprinkle with 3 tablespoons flour and cook, stirring, about 2 minutes, or until light brown.
7. Slowly add 1½ cups stock, whisking constantly to prevent lumps. When sauce is smooth, stir in Madeira, chopped tomato, marjoram, fennel seed, and salt and pepper to taste, and bring to a boil, stirring constantly.
8. Add enough sauce (about ½ cup) to chicken mixture to moisten well; reserve remaining sauce.
9. Turn chicken mixture into chilled shell. Cover with top crust, crimping edges of pastry together to seal. Cut 5 or 6 small leaf shapes from pastry trimmings and arrange decoratively in center of pie. Bake tourte 10 minutes.
10. In small bowl, beat egg with a fork. Remove tourte from oven and reduce temperature to 350 degrees. Brush top of crust with beaten egg to glaze and bake another 15 minutes, or until top is golden.
11. Just before serving, return reserved sauce to medium heat for 5 minutes, or until heated through. Pour sauce through strainer set over small pitcher or sauceboat.
12. Remove tourte from oven and serve with sauce.

Mixed Green Salad

Large head Boston lettuce
Large head red leaf lettuce
1 lemon
¼ cup plus 2 tablespoons extra-virgin olive oil
2 ounces Parmesan cheese
Salt and freshly ground black pepper

1. Wash lettuce and dry in salad spinner or pat dry with paper towels. Tear greens into bite-size pieces, place in salad bowl, cover with plastic wrap, and refrigerate until ready to serve.
2. Squeeze enough lemon to measure about 2 tablespoons juice. In small bowl, combine olive oil and lemon juice and beat vigorously with fork until blended; set aside.
3. Grate enough Parmesan to measure ½ cup; set aside.
4. Just before serving, beat dressing to recombine and pour over salad greens. Toss greens until evenly coated, season with salt and pepper to taste, and sprinkle generously with grated Parmesan.

ADDED TOUCH

This cake has a very moist, almost pudding-like texture. Use canned, unsweetened chestnut purée to save time or, if preferred, use canned peeled chestnuts.

Chestnut Cake

15½-ounce can unsweetened chestnut purée
1 cup heavy cream, plus 1 cup (optional)
⅓ cup walnut-flavored liqueur (Nociello or eau-de-noix)
2 sticks butter, at room temperature
1½ cups sugar
8 eggs, separated
¼ teaspoon cream of tartar
1 tablespoon maple syrup (optional)

1. Preheat oven to 375 degrees.
2. Butter and flour 10-inch springform pan. In medium-size saucepan, combine 2½ cups chestnut purée, 1 cup heavy cream, and liqueur, and bring to a simmer over medium heat. Set aside and allow to cool to room temperature.
3. In bowl of electric mixer, cream butter and 1 cup sugar. One at a time, add egg yolks to butter-sugar mixture, beating after each addition until thoroughly blended.
4. In another bowl, beat egg whites and cream of tartar until frothy. Still beating, slowly add remaining ½ cup sugar and continue to beat until whites are stiff but not dry.
5. With electric mixer at lowest setting, add chestnut purée to creamed butter-egg mixture and beat just until blended.
6. With a rubber spatula, fold egg whites quickly into chestnut batter. Turn mixture into springform pan, smooth top, and bake 1 hour and 20 minutes, or until cake is set but still slightly underdone in center. Allow to cool to room temperature before unmolding.
7. Just before serving, whip heavy cream and maple syrup with chilled beaters in chilled bowl until stiff. Unmold cake and serve garnished with maple-flavored whipped cream, if desired.

Sautéed Chicken Breasts with Vegetables and Summer Savory Butter
Aligot

White china emphasizes the colors and textures of this elegant meal: chicken with vegetables and potato aligot.

Carrots and parsnips, two characteristic Auvergnac vegetables, are usually available year round in American supermarkets. Summer savory, an easy-to-grow annual, has a robust, peppery taste, somewhat like that of thyme. Either fresh or dried savory will do for this recipe, and herb butter can be made ahead and stored for two or three weeks in the refrigerator. Incorporating an herb butter into a reduced stock, as in this recipe, makes the sauce shimmer and produces a very flavorful result. For the potato casserole, or *aligot*, use Cantal, a firm, strong cheese that is similar to sharp Cheddar—or substitute Cheddar, if necessary.

WHAT TO DRINK

An ideal wine for this dinner is a Gewürztraminer—a dry and spicy one from Alsace or a fruitier California version. Either will nicely enrich the sauce for the chicken breasts.

SHOPPING LIST AND STAPLES

4 skinless, boneless chicken breasts (about 3 pounds total weight)
½ pound lean ham, unsliced
3 large boiling potatoes (about 1¼ pounds total weight)
½ pound parsnips
½ pound carrots
1 to 2 large shallots
2 cloves garlic
1 bunch scallions
Small bunch fresh parsley
Small bunch fresh summer savory, or 2 teaspoons dried
1 lemon
2 sticks plus 5 tablespoons unsalted butter
¼ pound Cantal or sharp Cheddar cheese
1 cup chicken stock, preferably homemade (see page 11), or canned
1 teaspoon ground coriander
Salt
Freshly ground black pepper
½ cup dry white wine

UTENSILS

Food processor (optional)
Electric mixer (if not using processor)
Large heavy-gauge skillet
Medium-size heavy-gauge skillet with cover
Medium-size saucepan with cover
Small heavy-gauge saucepan or butter warmer
Flameproof baking dish
Medium-size bowl (if not using processor)
Small bowls
Colander
Measuring cups and spoons
Chef's knife
Paring knife
Wooden spoon
Large spoon
Wooden spatula
Potato masher (if not using processor)
Tongs
Vegetable peeler
Juicer (optional)
Grater (if not using processor)
Meat pounder or rolling pin

START-TO-FINISH STEPS

One hour ahead: For summer savory butter, set out 1 stick plus 4 tablespoons butter to bring to room temperature.

Fifteen minutes ahead: Clarify 3 tablespoons of butter for chicken recipe.

1. For savory butter and aligot, wash parsley and summer savory, and pat dry. Chop enough parsley to measure 4 tablespoons and enough savory to measure 1 tablespoon. Peel and mince garlic and shallots.
2. Follow savory butter recipe step 1.
3. Follow aligot recipe steps 1 and 2.
4. Follow chicken recipe step 1.
5. Follow aligot recipe steps 3 through 5.
6. Follow chicken recipe steps 2 and 3.
7. While vegetables are cooking, follow savory butter recipe steps 2 through 4.
8. Follow chicken recipe steps 4 through 9 and aligot recipe step 6.
9. Follow chicken recipe step 10 and serve with aligot.

RECIPES

Sautéed Chicken Breasts with Vegetables and Summer Savory Butter

4 skinless, boneless chicken breasts (about 3 pounds total weight)
½ pound parsnips
½ pound carrots
3 tablespoons unsalted butter plus 3 tablespoons, clarified
Freshly ground black pepper
2 tablespoons chopped fresh parsley
½ cup dry white wine
1 cup chicken stock, preferably homemade (see page 11), or canned
⅔ cup Summer Savory Butter (see following recipe)

1. Trim chicken breasts of any excess fat and cartilage. With meat pounder or rolling pin, gently flatten breasts to about ½-inch thickness. Split breasts in half, place between two layers of paper towels, and pat dry. Set aside.
2. Peel parsnips and halve lengthwise. Lay parsnip halves flat sides down and cut on diagonal into ½-inch-thick slices. Peel and cut carrots as for parsnips. Set vegetables aside.
3. In medium-size heavy-gauge skillet, melt 3 tablespoons

butter over medium heat. When butter stops sizzling but before it browns, add parsnip and carrot slices, stirring to coat evenly with butter. Reduce heat to medium-low and cook, turning occasionally, about 5 minutes, or until vegetables are brown at the edges. Season with pepper to taste and sprinkle with 1 tablespoon chopped parsley. Cover skillet and set aside.

4. Preheat oven to 200 degrees.

5. Heat large heavy-gauge skillet over medium-high heat. Add clarified butter and, just as it begins to smoke, add chicken breasts, smooth side down. Sauté chicken about 3 minutes, or until brown on one side. With tongs, turn chicken, tilt skillet to redistribute butter evenly in pan, and sauté on second side about 2 minutes. Turn chicken and continue to cook, turning, until meat in center is still slightly pink and moist, another 2 to 5 minutes.

6. Divide chicken among individual dinner plates and keep warm in oven until ready to serve.

7. Reduce heat to medium, add ½ cup dry white wine, and deglaze pan by scraping up any browned bits clinging to bottom. Increase heat to high and cook until wine is reduced by half, about 3 minutes. Add stock to pan and reduce liquid again by half, about 3 minutes.

8. Remove skillet from heat. One tablespoon at a time, stir in ⅔ cup of prepared summer savory butter. When butter has been totally incorporated, pour just enough sauce over vegetables to coat them.

9. Remove dinner plates from oven and turn on broiler.

10. Spoon remaining sauce over chicken breast halves. Spoon carrots and parsnips around chicken, sprinkle with remaining chopped parsley, and serve.

Summer Savory Butter

1 lemon
1 tablespoon minced fresh summer savory, or 2 teaspoons dried
1 stick plus 4 tablespoons unsalted butter
1 to 2 large shallots, peeled and minced
1 clove garlic, peeled and minced
2 tablespoons chopped fresh parsley

1. Squeeze lemon and set juice aside. If using dried summer savory, combine with lemon juice in small bowl to allow herb flavor to develop.

2. Using food processor or electric mixer and bowl, cream butter until smooth.

3. Add shallots, garlic, parsley, and summer savory to butter and beat just until blended.

4. One teaspoon at a time, add lemon juice, or lemon juice with dried summer savory, if using, and beat until blended. Turn herb butter into small bowl, cover, and refrigerate until ready to use.

Aligot

3 large boiling potatoes (about 1¼ pounds total weight)
Salt
3 tablespoons unsalted butter
1 bunch scallions

¼ pound Cantal or sharp Cheddar cheese
½ pound lean ham
1 clove garlic, peeled and minced
1 teaspoon ground coriander

1. Peel potatoes and cut into 1½-inch cubes. In medium-size saucepan, bring potatoes, 1 teaspoon salt, and water to cover to a boil over high heat. Lower heat to medium and boil, covered, 10 to 12 minutes, or until tender.

2. Meanwhile, melt butter in small heavy-gauge saucepan or butter warmer over low heat. Wash scallions and pat dry. Trim ends and cut enough scallions into ¼-inch-thick pieces to measure 1 cup. Grate cheese in processor or on coarse side of grater. Slice ham into ½-inch-thick cubes.

3. Drain potatoes of all but 2 to 3 tablespoons of liquid. In food processor or with potato masher, mash coarsely.

4. Add cheese, ham, garlic, coriander, and all but 2 tablespoons scallions to potatoes, and stir until combined.

5. Turn potatoes into flameproof serving dish and sprinkle with melted butter and remaining scallions. Cover with foil and keep warm.

6. Just before serving, brown under broiler for 2 minutes.

ADDED TOUCH

Highly aromatic cardamom adds an elusive spiciness to this chocolate cake.

Chocolate Pecan Cake

1 orange
2½-ounce can pecan pieces
1 ounce (1 square) semisweet chocolate, grated
5 eggs
¼ cup plus 2 tablespoons sugar
2 tablespoons Dutch-processed unsweetened cocoa powder
½ teaspoon almond extract
1 teaspoon cardamom

1. Preheat oven to 350 degrees.

2. Grate zest of orange, being careful to avoid white pith. In food processor or with nut grinder, finely grind enough pecans to measure ¾ cup. In food processor or on coarse side of grater, grate chocolate.

3. Separate 4 eggs, placing yolks in large mixing bowl and whites in medium-size bowl. Add remaining whole egg and ¼ cup sugar to yolks, and, with electric mixer at high speed, beat until thick, about 10 minutes. Rinse and dry beaters.

4. Beat egg whites until frothy. Gradually add remaining sugar and continue beating until whites form soft peaks. Set aside.

5. To yolk mixture, add grated chocolate, cocoa, ground pecans, almond extract, orange zest, and cardamom, and stir until blended.

6. Gently fold whites into yolk mixture and turn into buttered and floured 8½ x 4¼ x 3-inch loaf pan. Bake about 40 minutes, or until a toothpick inserted in the center comes out clean. Cool in pan before turning out onto rack.

Veal Scallops with Saffron Apples
Lentils with Tomatoes and Bacon
Sorrel and Celery Root Salad

Saffron-tinted apple slices contrast handsomely with veal scallops for this Auvergnac-style meal. Serve the tossed sorrel and celery root salad and the lentils with tomatoes and bacon in separate wooden bowls.

The sautéed veal scallops cook through quickly if you gently flatten them to a uniform thickness. Ask your butcher for veal scallops, cut from the loin, that are almost white. Make sure they are trimmed of any fat or silvery membrane. Before sautéeing the scallops, pat them dry so the butter does not spatter when you place them in the pan. To seal in the juices, avoid overcrowding the pieces.

The sauce for the veal contains *crème fraîche* and saffron, the world's costliest spice. *Crème fraîche* is a thickened cultured cream product with a slightly tart nutty taste. At one time available only in France, *crème fraîche* is now found in some American supermarkets and in specialty food shops. To make your own, follow the directions on page 72. Both the green and the red lentils called for in the warm salad are imports, usually available at health food stores only. Regular supermarket lentils are acceptable, if not quite as flavorful and attractive.

Both the sorrel and celery root, or celeriac, in the salad are typically French vegetables. Sorrel, or sour grass, is a tart perennial herb that resembles spinach. If you substitute spinach, increase the amount of lemon juice and vinegar in the dressing to 1 tablespoon each. Celery root tastes a bit like nutty celery. Buy it no larger than 4 inches in diameter or the flesh will be woody. Since the skin is very thick, you will trim away almost half of the root when you peel it.

WHAT TO DRINK

A full-bodied white Burgundy would be a perfect accompaniment for this meal. A good-quality California Chardonnay would also be excellent.

SHOPPING LIST AND STAPLES

8 to 12 veal scallops (about 1½ pounds total weight)
½ pound smoked slab bacon, unsliced
2 large tomatoes (about 1¼ pounds total weight)
1 cucumber
1 celery root (about 1½ pounds)
Large red bell pepper
Small onion
¾ pound fresh sorrel or spinach
Small bunch parsley
1 to 2 large shallots
3 cloves garlic
Large lemon

4 medium-size tart apples, preferably Northern Spy, Cortland, or Granny Smith (about 2 pounds total weight)
1 cup crème fraîche or heavy cream
1 stick unsalted butter
2 ounces Parmesan cheese
½ cup veal or chicken stock, preferably homemade (see page 11), or canned
¼ cup plus 2 tablespoons olive oil
2 teaspoons tarragon vinegar
2 tablespoons Dijon mustard
1 tablespoon anchovy paste
¾ pound green or red lentils
½ cup flour for dredging
1 teaspoon dry mustard
½ teaspoon dried rosemary
½ teaspoon dried sage
1 teaspoon saffron threads
Salt
Freshly ground black pepper
⅓ cup dry white wine plus ¼ cup dry white vermouth, or about ½ cup dry white vermouth

UTENSILS

Large heavy-gauge skillet or sauté pan
Medium-size heavy-gauge skillet or saucepan
Medium-size heavy-gauge saucepan with cover
2 small saucepans
9-inch pie pan
Heatproof serving platter
Large flat plate
Wooden salad bowl
Heatproof serving bowl
Large mixing bowl
Small bowl
Colander
Large sieve
Salad spinner (optional)
Measuring cups and spoons
Chef's knife
Paring knife
Large spoon
Slotted metal spatula
Wooden spatula
Tongs
Melon baller or teaspoon
Vegetable peeler
Grater
Juicer (optional)
Wooden mallet or rolling pin
Small jar with tight-fitting lid

START-TO-FINISH STEPS

The day before: If making your own crème fraîche, combine ½ pint heavy cream and ½ pint sour cream at room temperature in small bowl and whisk until blended. Turn into glass jar, cover tightly, and let stand at room temperature 6 to 8 hours. Refrigerate until ready to use.

One hour ahead: For lentils recipe, set out 2 tablespoons butter to reach room temperature.

Fifteen minutes ahead: Clarify 6 tablespoons butter (see page 10) for veal.

1. Follow salad recipe steps 1 through 5.
2. Follow lentils recipe steps 1 through 4.
3. While tomato mixture is simmering, follow veal recipe steps 1 through 3.
4. Follow lentils recipe steps 5 through 7.
5. While lentils are simmering, follow salad recipe steps 6 through 8.
6. Follow lentils recipe step 8 and veal recipe steps 4 through 7.
7. Follow salad recipe step 9, veal recipe step 8, and serve with lentils.

RECIPES

Veal Scallops with Saffron Apples

Large lemon
4 medium-size tart apples, preferably Northern Spy, Cortland, or Granny Smith (about 2 pounds total weight)
1 to 2 large shallots
2 cloves garlic
1 teaspoon saffron threads
8 to 12 veal scallops (about 1½ pounds total weight)
½ cup flour for dredging
6 tablespoons unsalted butter, clarified
⅓ cup dry white wine or dry white vermouth
½ cup veal or chicken stock, preferably homemade (see page 11), or canned
1 cup crème fraîche or heavy cream

1. Preheat oven to 200 degrees.
2. Squeeze lemon, reserving 2 teaspoons juice for salad dressing. Wash, halve, and core apples; cut into ¼-inch-thick wedges. Peel and mince enough shallots to measure ¼ cup. Peel and mince garlic. Combine apples, lemon juice, shallots, garlic, and saffron in large mixing bowl and toss to combine; set aside.
3. Trim veal of any fat or membrane. With a wooden mallet or rolling pin, flatten, but do not pound, veal scallops to a uniform thickness of about ¼ inch.
4. Place ½ cup flour in pie pan and lightly dredge veal scallops on both sides. Shake off excess flour and set aside on large flat plate.
5. In large heavy-gauge skillet, heat 3 to 4 tablespoons clarified butter over medium-high heat. Place as many scallops in skillet as will fit without overcrowding, increase heat to high, and brown veal quickly, 2 to 3 minutes on each side, adding more clarified butter as needed. With tongs, transfer scallops to heatproof serving platter and keep warm in oven. Repeat for remaining scallops.
6. For sauce, carefully pour off any fat and butter remain-

ing in skillet. Add ⅓ cup wine and deglaze pan over medium-high heat, scraping up any browned bits clinging to bottom of pan with a wooden spatula. Cook until liquid is reduced to 2 tablespoons, about 2 minutes. Add veal or chicken stock. From serving platter, pour accumulated veal juices back into skillet. Increase heat to high and cook, stirring, until sauce is reduced to ¼ cup, about 2 minutes.

7. Add crème fraîche, or heavy cream, to reduced stock, and cook at just under boiling point until sauce thickens, 3 to 5 minutes.

8. Add apple mixture to sauce and stir gently until combined. Reduce heat and simmer gently until apples are heated through, about 2 minutes. Pour sauce over veal scallops, top with apples, and serve immediately.

Lentils with Tomatoes and Bacon

¾ pound green or red lentils (about 1½ cups)
Salt
½ pound smoked slab bacon, unsliced
Small onion
2 large tomatoes
½ teaspoon dried sage
½ teaspoon dried rosemary
¼ cup dry white vermouth
Small bunch parsley
2 tablespoons unsalted butter

1. Pick over lentils to remove pebbles or other foreign matter. Place lentils in large sieve and rinse thoroughly under cold running water. Transfer to medium-size heavy-gauge saucepan. Add ½ teaspoon salt and water to cover, and bring to a boil over high heat, skimming off any scum that rises to surface.

2. While lentils are coming to a boil, slice bacon into ½-inch cubes, about 1¼ cups. Peel and chop enough onion to measure ⅓ cup. Wash tomatoes and pat dry. Peel, core, halve, seed, and chop tomatoes; set aside.

3. Boil lentils 1 minute, cover, and remove from heat.

4. In medium-size heavy-gauge skillet, fry bacon cubes over medium heat until crisp, about 5 minutes. Add onion and sauté until onion is translucent, about 3 minutes. Carefully pour off bacon fat from skillet. Add tomatoes, sage, rosemary, and vermouth, and simmer until nearly all liquid has evaporated, about 15 minutes. Set aside.

5. In large sieve, drain lentils and rinse under cold running water. Return lentils to saucepan, add fresh water to cover by 1 inch, and bring lentils to a boil over high heat.

6. While lentils are coming to a boil, wash parsley and pat dry with paper towels. Chop enough parsley to measure 2 tablespoons.

7. Lower heat under lentils to a simmer, cover, and cook gently until tender, about 10 minutes for green lentils or 4 minutes for red lentils.

8. Transfer lentils to sieve, drain thoroughly, and turn into heatproof serving bowl. Add bacon-tomato mixture, butter, and chopped parsley, and toss gently to combine. Keep warm in 200-degree oven until ready to serve.

Sorrel and Celery Root Salad

¼ cup plus 2 tablespoons olive oil
2 teaspoons tarragon vinegar
2 teaspoons lemon juice
2 teaspoons Dijon mustard
1 teaspoon dry mustard
1 tablespoon anchovy paste
1 cucumber
Large red bell pepper
1 celery root (about 1½ pounds)
¾ pound fresh sorrel or spinach
1 clove garlic
2 ounces Parmesan cheese
Salt and freshly ground black pepper

1. For dressing, combine olive oil, vinegar, lemon juice, mustards, and anchovy paste in small jar with tight-fitting lid, and shake until thoroughly blended. Set aside at room temperature.

2. Peel cucumber, halve lengthwise, and scrape out seeds with teaspoon or melon baller. Cut halves into ½-inch-thick crescents. Place in colander, sprinkle with 1 tablespoon salt, and set aside to drain.

3. Wash red pepper and pat dry. Core, seed, and cut pepper into 1-inch squares. Place pepper in small bowl, drizzle with 2 to 3 tablespoons dressing, toss gently, and set aside.

4. In small saucepan, bring 1 quart of water to a boil over high heat. While water is heating, peel celery root and cut in half. Cut halves into ¼-inch-thick slices, then into julienne strips. Plunge celery root into boiling water and blanch 10 seconds. Transfer to sieve and refresh under cold running water. Drain thoroughly, wrap in paper towels, and refrigerate until ready to assemble salad.

5. Wash sorrel, or spinach, if using, and remove any discolored leaves. Dry in salad spinner or pat dry with paper towels. Wrap in paper towels and refrigerate.

6. Peel garlic clove and rub over inside surface of wooden salad bowl. Discard garlic. Cover bowl and set aside.

7. In food processor or with grater, grate enough Parmesan to measure 2 tablespoons.

8. Rinse cucumber under cold running water to remove salt. Place in cloth napkin or kitchen towel and squeeze out any excess moisture. Add cucumbers to peppers and toss.

9. Place sorrel and celery root in salad bowl. Shake dressing to recombine, pour over sorrel and celery root, and toss. Top with peppers and cucumbers, sprinkle with Parmesan, and season with black pepper to taste.

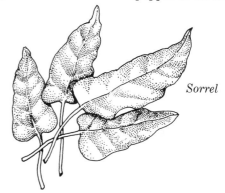

Sorrel

Jill Van Cleave and William Rice

Jill Van Cleave and William Rice favor straight-forward, no-nonsense meals that do not overtax the cook. "We never attempt culinary feats when we prepare meals for company," he says. "Our party food is what we would cook for ourselves, that is, food with character." As a cooking team, they also share the shopping, the prepping, and the table setting, which they consider as important as the meal itself.

Having traveled extensively in France, the couple selected menus that highlighted their favorite regional dishes, which they have adapted to their own tastes. For instance, the first course of Menu 1, a cold-weather Burgundian meal, combines two of the region's specialties: snails (*escargots*) and Burgundy wine. Rather than lavishing the snails with butter, as in the traditional *escargots à la bourguignonne*, the cooks have devised a garlic-scented wine sauce, and they serve the snails on croutons rather than in their shells. The entrée consists of thick pork chops in a Dijon mustard sauce.

Menu 2, a company lunch or dinner, includes three typical Lyonnaise dishes: a salad of tart greens and bits of bacon, an entrée of chicken flavored with garlic and vinegar, and, for dessert, rich *pots de crème* that combine chocolate and chestnuts.

For Menu 3, a Gascony meal, the cooks offer broiled duck breasts garnished with prunes simmered in Armagnac, Gascony's own renowned brandy. Mashed potatoes flavored with garlic accompany the main course.

Offer your guests the snails in red Burgundy wine sauce either with the main course or as an appetizer. Just before serving the entrée, spoon some sauce over each pork chop and sprinkle generously with chive slivers. The carrots are glazed and then rolled in minced parsley.

75

Snails in Burgundy Wine Sauce
Pork Chops Dijonnaise
Glazed Carrots

In France, snails are a gastronomic prize and snail hunting a national pastime. Canned snails, without shells or with separately packed shells, are available in specialty food shops and many supermarkets.

Dijon mustard, used in the sauce for the pork chops, is a type of mustard named for the principal city of Burgundy. It is made from ground mustard seeds, white wine, and a variety of seasonings.

WHAT TO DRINK

A good red Burgundy is the obvious partner for this meal. Try a Côte de Nuits or a Côte de Beaune-Villages.

SHOPPING LIST AND STAPLES

Four ¾- to 1-inch-thick center-cut loin pork chops (about 2 pounds total weight)
2 slices bacon
1½ pounds carrots
Small onion
Large clove garlic
Small bunch parsley
Small bunch chives
4 tablespoons unsalted butter
Two 7½-ounce cans giant snails without shells
½ cup chicken stock, preferably homemade (see page 11), or canned
16-ounce can tomato purée
1 tablespoon vegetable oil
2 tablespoons Dijon mustard
⅔ cup flour, approximately
4 slices home-style white bread
1½ teaspoons sugar
Salt and freshly ground black pepper
1 cup red Burgundy wine
½ cup dry white Burgundy wine
1 tablespoon brandy

UTENSILS

Large skillet
2 medium-size saucepans, one with cover
13 x 9 x 2-inch baking dish
13 x 9-inch cookie sheet
Small bowl
Measuring cups and spoons
Chef's knife
Paring knife
2 wooden spoons
Metal tongs
3-inch round pastry cutter (optional)
Small whisk
Vegetable peeler

START-TO-FINISH STEPS

One hour ahead: For snails recipe, set out 2 tablespoons butter to bring to room temperature.

1. Wash parsley and chives, and pat dry with paper towels. Reserve 4 parsley sprigs for snails, if using for garnish, and chop 2 tablespoons for carrots. For pork chops, chop 2 tablespoons chives and sliver 2 tablespoons, if using for garnish.
2. Follow snails recipe steps 1 through 5.
3. While bacon is browning, follow carrots recipe step 1.
4. Follow snails recipe step 6 and pork chops recipe steps 1 and 2.
5. While pork chops are browning, follow snails recipe step 7 and carrots recipe step 2.
6. While snails are simmering, follow pork chops recipe step 3.
7. Follow snails recipe step 8 and carrots recipe steps 3 and 4.
8. Follow snails recipe steps 9 and 10, and serve as a first course.
9. Follow pork chops recipe step 4 and remove carrots from heat.
10. Follow pork chops recipe step 5 and carrots recipe step 5.
11. Follow pork chops recipe steps 6 and 7, and serve with carrots.

RECIPES

Snails in Burgundy Wine Sauce

4 slices home-style white bread
Small onion
Large garlic clove
2 slices bacon
1 cup red Burgundy wine
½ cup chicken stock
1 tablespoon brandy
Salt and freshly ground black pepper
Two 7½-ounce cans giant snails without shells

2 tablespoons unsalted butter
2 tablespoons flour
4 sprigs parsley for garnish (optional)

1. Preheat oven to 350 degrees.
2. With a pastry cutter or paring knife, cut out a 3-inch-round crouton from each slice of bread. Arrange croutons in a single layer on cookie sheet and toast in oven 5 minutes, or until lightly brown.
3. Meanwhile, peel and mince onion and garlic. Dice bacon.
4. Transfer toasted croutons to 4 small soup bowls or salad plates.
5. In medium-size saucepan, cook bacon 3 to 5 minutes, or until browned.
6. Add onion and garlic, and cook another 3 to 5 minutes, or until onion is translucent.
7. Add red wine, stock, brandy, and salt and pepper to taste, and bring to a boil over medium heat. Rinse and drain snails, and add to liquid in pan. Reduce heat to low and simmer snails 5 minutes.
8. With metal tongs, transfer snails to medium-size bowl, cover with foil and keep warm.
9. In small bowl, blend butter with flour until smooth. Add butter-flour mixture to sauce all at once, whisking until blended, and cook, stirring, about 3 minutes, or until thick and smooth. Remove pan from heat.
10. Divide snails among bowls or plates containing croutons, top each with a few spoonfuls of sauce, and serve garnished with a parsley sprig, if desired.

Pork Chops Dijonnaise

Four ¾- to 1-inch-thick center-cut loin pork chops (about 2 pounds total weight)
¼ cup flour, approximately
1 tablespoon vegetable oil
Salt and freshly ground pepper
½ cup dry white Burgundy wine
2 tablespoons Dijon mustard
1 tablespoon tomato purée
2 tablespoons chopped chives plus 2 tablespoons slivered chives for garnish (optional)

1. Press pork chops between 2 layers of paper towels to absorb moisture. Place flour on sheet of waxed paper. Lightly dredge chops in flour; shake off excess.
2. In large skillet, heat oil over medium-high heat. Add chops and brown 4 to 5 minutes per side.

3. Season chops with salt and pepper to taste, and transfer to shallow baking dish. Bake in 350-degree oven 15 minutes.
4. Pour off fat from skillet. Add wine, mustard, tomato purée, and chopped chives to skillet, and stir sauce over medium heat, scraping up any browned particles clinging to bottom of pan. Reduce heat to low and simmer sauce, stirring often, 5 minutes. Turn off heat under skillet.
5. Divide baked chops among individual dinner plates and lower oven temperature to 200 degrees, leaving oven door ajar a few moments to hasten cooling. Return chops to oven and keep warm.
6. Add juices that have accumulated in baking pan to sauce in skillet. Reheat sauce over medium heat until bubbly; turn off heat and season with salt and pepper to taste.
7. Top each chop with a few spoonfuls of sauce and garnish with chive slivers, if desired.

Glazed Carrots

1½ pounds carrots
2 tablespoons unsalted butter
1½ teaspoons sugar
¼ teaspoon salt
2 tablespoons chopped parsley

1. Peel and trim carrots. Cut into 2-inch-long pieces of approximately uniform thickness.
2. In medium-size saucepan, melt butter over medium heat. Add carrots and cook, turning often, 3 to 5 minutes.
3. Sprinkle carrots with sugar and salt, and continue cooking another 3 minutes.
4. Pour ½ cup warm water over carrots, raise heat to high, and bring to a boil. Reduce heat to medium, cover, and cook at a brisk simmer, 10 to 15 minutes, or until carrots are tender but still firm when pricked with the point of a knife. Remove pan from heat.
5. About 5 minutes before serving, reheat carrots, uncovered, over high heat until liquid has reduced to a glaze. Sprinkle with chopped parsley and turn carrots until evenly coated. Remove pan from heat.

LEFTOVER SUGGESTION

Any leftover cooked carrots can be used in many ways: mash them and reheat them with crème fraîche, or purée them to thicken sauces or soups. Try stirring puréed carrots into bread dough for extra moistness.

Chicken with Garlic-Vinegar Sauce
Lyonnaise Salad
Chocolate Pots de Crème with Chestnuts

Chicken with garlic-vinegar sauce and a green salad are ideal buffet fare. Serve the chilled pots de crème *in individual ramekins.*

Most supermarket vinegars are too harsh and acidic for this chicken recipe. If you cannot find imported natural red Burgundy wine vinegar in your local gourmet shop, dilute regular vinegar by mixing it half and half with the wine suggested for this meal.

The chocolate *pots de crème* are so-called because they are traditionally served in small lidded porcelain pots.

WHAT TO DRINK

This menu can be paired with either a white or a red wine. For white, choose a crisp, dry California Sauvignon Blanc. For red, opt for a light and fruity French Beaujolais.

SHOPPING LIST AND STAPLES

2½- to 3-pound chicken, cut into 12 serving pieces
¼ to ½ pound thick-cut bacon (4 to 6 slices)
2 medium-size tomatoes (¾ to 1 pound total weight), or 16-ounce can Italian plum
1 head chicory
1 head escarole
Small bunch scallions (optional)
Small bunch parsley
4 large cloves garlic plus 1 clove (if making croutons)
5 eggs
½ pint heavy cream
4 tablespoons unsalted butter
15½-ounce can whole chestnuts, preferably water-packed
½ cup chicken stock, preferably homemade (see page 11), or canned
½ cup vegetable oil
½ cup olive oil (if making croutons)
¾ cup red wine vinegar, preferably natural red Burgundy wine vinegar
2 teaspoons Dijon mustard
1½ teaspoons vanilla extract
1 large loaf French bread or baguette (if making croutons)
1 cup croutons, ½-inch-thick (if not using homemade)
4 squares sweet chocolate (4 ounces)
2 tablespoons sugar
Salt and freshly ground pepper

UTENSILS

Electric mixer
Large deep skillet or flameproof casserole with cover
Small skillet
Small heavy-gauge saucepan
Salad bowl
Large bowl
Small bowl
Salad spinner (optional)
Measuring cups and spoons
Chef's knife
Paring knife
2 wooden spoons
Metal spoon
Slotted spatula
Whisk
Metal tongs
4 ramekins, or porcelain *pots de crème*

START-TO-FINISH STEPS

At least two hours ahead: For chocolate *pots de crème*, follow steps 1 to 4.

Ahead of time: To make homemade croutons for salad, cut four ½-inch slices from large loaf of French bread or eight ½-inch slices from baguette into ½-inch dice. In heavy-gauge skillet, heat ½ cup olive oil over medium-high heat. Add peeled and minced garlic clove (or more to taste), stir, and add bread. Fry briefly, stirring, until bread is golden, about 1 to 2 minutes. Transfer croutons to paper towels to drain.

1. Follow chicken recipe step 1 and salad recipe steps 1 through 3.
2. Follow chicken recipe steps 2 through 4.
3. Follow salad recipe steps 4 and 5.
4. Follow chicken recipe step 5 and serve with salad.
5. Follow pots de crème recipe step 5 and serve for dessert.

RECIPES

Chicken with Garlic-Vinegar Sauce

2 medium-size tomatoes (¾ to 1 pound total weight), or 16-ounce Italian plum
Small bunch parsley
4 tablespoons unsalted butter
1 tablespoon vegetable oil
4 large cloves garlic
2½- to 3-pound chicken, cut into 12 serving pieces
Salt and freshly ground pepper

¼ cup plus 1 tablespoon red wine vinegar, preferably natural red Burgundy wine vinegar
½ cup chicken stock

1. If using fresh tomatoes, peel, core, halve, and seed. If using canned tomatoes, drain. Coarsely chop tomatoes and set aside. Wash parsley, pat dry with paper towels, and chop enough to measure 3 tablespoons. Refrigerate remaining parsley in plastic bag for another use.

2. In large deep skillet or flameproof casserole that will hold chicken in a single layer, combine 2 tablespoons butter, oil, and 4 unpeeled cloves garlic over medium-high heat. When butter stops foaming, add chicken pieces, and sauté, turning once, until pieces are lightly browned, about 5 minutes. Season chicken with salt and pepper to taste.

3. Add ¼ cup vinegar to skillet and bring to a boil. Add tomatoes, stock, and 2 tablespoons of chopped parsley, and, with wooden spoon, scrape up browned bits clinging to bottom of pan. When liquid returns to a boil, cover skillet, reduce heat to low, and simmer, turning chicken pieces once, about 15 minutes.

4. Transfer chicken to serving dish and cover loosely with foil to keep warm.

5. Remove garlic cloves from skillet and push cloves out of skins. Mince cloves and return to skillet. Mash garlic with wooden spoon. Add remaining tablespoon vinegar and simmer liquid over medium heat, stirring constantly, until reduced by one third. Remove pan from heat, cover, and keep warm.

6. Add salt and pepper to taste. Return skillet to heat, add remaining 2 tablespoons butter, and whisk until sauce is smooth and heated through. Pour sauce over chicken and garnish with remaining chopped parsley.

Lyonnaise Salad

1 head escarole
1 head chicory
1 cup croutons, ½-inch thick, preferably homemade
2 teaspoons Dijon mustard
¼ cup plus 2 tablespoons red wine vinegar
¼ to ½ pound thick-cut bacon (4 to 6 slices)
¼ cup plus 2 tablespoons vegetable oil
Small bunch scallions (optional)
Salt and freshly ground pepper

1. Wash greens and dry in salad spinner or pat dry with paper towels. Tear into bite-size pieces and combine with croutons in salad bowl. If using scallions, wash and pat dry. Finely chop white part of 2 scallions and set aside; reserve remaining whole scallions and green parts for another use.

2. Combine mustard and vinegar in small bowl and whisk until blended; set aside.

3. Cut bacon strips crosswise into ½-inch pieces to make about 1 cup. In small skillet, cook bacon over medium heat until fat is rendered and pieces are brown, about 5 minutes. With slotted spatula, transfer bacon to paper towels to drain; add to salad bowl.

4. Pour off all but about 2 tablespoons drippings from skillet. Add vegetable oil and stir until blended. To avoid spattering, remove skillet from heat and carefully add mustard-vinegar mixture. Return skillet to medium heat and bring liquid just to a boil. Remove from heat, stir, and pour over salad.

5. Season salad with salt and pepper to taste, toss, and sprinkle with scallions.

Chocolate Pots de Crème with Chestnuts

15½-ounce can whole chestnuts, preferably water-packed
5 eggs
4 squares sweet chocolate (4 ounces)
1 cup heavy cream
2 tablespoons sugar
Pinch of salt
1½ teaspoons vanilla extract

1. Drain chestnuts and coarsely chop enough to measure ½ cup. Slice 2 chestnuts in half for garnish, if desired. Separate eggs, placing yolks in large bowl and reserving whites for another use.

2. In small heavy-gauge saucepan, combine chocolate and heavy cream, and bring just to a boil, stirring frequently with wooden spoon, over medium heat. Remove pan from heat immediately.

3. Add sugar and a pinch of salt to yolks, and beat with an electric mixer at high speed until eggs thicken. Slowly add scalded chocolate cream, stirring constantly to avoid cooking egg yolks or curdling cream mixture. Stir in vanilla and fold in chopped chestnuts.

4. Divide mixture among 4 small ramekins or porcelain pots de crème without lids and refrigerate until set, at least 2 hours.

5. When ready to serve, remove from refrigerator and garnish each ramekin with a chestnut half, if desired.

Broiled Duck Breast with Prunes in Armagnac
Garlic Potatoes

Slices of duck breast with prunes simmered in brandy and garlic-rich mashed potatoes make an elegant company dinner.

Broiled duck breast with prunes in Armagnac is a dramatic entrée for an informal meal. Most supermarkets sell frozen whole ducks, but you may sometimes find fresh whole ducks or packaged fresh duck breast (the meaty part of the bird) as well.

Mashed potatoes redolent of garlic accompany the duck. The recipe suggests keeping the potatoes warm in their cooking water until you are ready to mash them; this adds flavor and eliminates possible scorching if you need to reheat the potatoes before mashing.

WHAT TO DRINK

The best accompaniment for this menu would be a good claret, such as a Saint-Estèphe, Saint-Julien, Pauillac, or one from another commune.

SHOPPING LIST AND STAPLES

2 boneless duck breasts (about 2 pounds total weight), or
  2 whole ducks
4 Idaho potatoes (about 1¾ pounds total weight)
10 cloves garlic
Small bunch parsley
½ pint heavy cream (optional)
4 tablespoons unsalted butter
½ cup beef stock, preferably homemade, or canned
8-ounce box pitted prunes
1 teaspoon dried thyme
Salt and freshly ground pepper
½ cup Armagnac or Cognac

UTENSILS

Large saucepan with cover
Small saucepan with cover
Broiler pan
Medium-size bowl
Small bowl
Food mill, ricer, or potato masher
Measuring cups and spoons
Chef's knife
Boning knife
Ladle
Wooden spoon
Metal tongs
Vegetable peeler

START-TO-FINISH STEPS

1. Follow duck recipe steps 1 through 4.
2. Follow potatoes recipe steps 1 and 2.
3. While pototoes are boiling, follow prunes recipe step 1.
4. While prunes are simmering, follow duck recipe step 5.
5. Follow potatoes recipe step 3.
6. Follow prunes recipe step 2, duck recipe step 6, and serve with garlic potatoes.

RECIPES

Broiled Duck Breast with Prunes in Armagnac

2 boneless duck breasts (about 2 pounds total weight), or
  2 whole ducks
2 cloves garlic
Small bunch parsley
1 teaspoon dried thyme
Salt and freshly ground pepper
Prunes in Armagnac (see following recipe)

1. Split boneless duck breasts in half and pat dry with paper towels. If using whole ducks, with a sharp boning knife, remove wings as close to bone as possible in order to leave maximum amount of meat on breast. Remove drumsticks and reserve with wings for another use. To separate breast from carcass, locate breastbone and make incision the length of the ridge (see illustration). Holding knife against breastbone and away from flesh, cut downward to

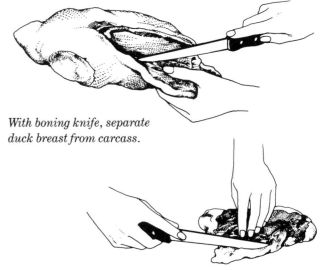

With boning knife, separate duck breast from carcass.

Trim away excess fat.

remove each breast section in one piece. Place each section skin side down and trim away excess fat, leaving skin intact, so that you have four half-heart-shaped pieces. Make ¼-inch-deep slashes in skin side of breast pieces.

2. Set broiler rack about 4 inches from heating element and preheat broiler. Peel garlic and mince enough to measure 1 teaspoon. Wash parsley, pat dry with paper towels, and chop enough to measure 1 teaspoon.

3. In small bowl, blend together garlic, parsley, thyme, ½ teaspoon salt, and pepper to taste.

4. Rub both sides of breast pieces with seasoning mixture. If not broiling immediately, let duck stand at room temperature.

5. Place breasts, skin side up, on broiler pan and broil 5 minutes. Turn breasts and broil 2 minutes more, or until centers of breasts are pink and juicy. Remove pan from broiler, cover with foil to keep warm, and set aside.

6. With chef's knife, slice each half breast across grain into 4 slices. Transfer to dinner plates and garnish each serving with 4 prunes and cooking liquid, and serve.

Prunes in Armagnac

8-ounce box pitted prunes
½ cup Armagnac or Cognac
½ cup beef stock, preferably homemade, or canned
Salt and freshly ground pepper

1. In small saucepan, combine prunes, Armagnac and stock. Bring to a slow simmer over low heat and cook 20 minutes, or until prunes are soft. Remove pan from heat, season with salt and pepper to taste, and cover to keep warm.

2. Just before serving, reheat prunes in liquid, if necessary.

Garlic Potatoes

4 Idaho potatoes (about 1¾ pounds total weight)
8 cloves garlic
Salt
4 tablespoons unsalted butter
¼ cup heavy cream (optional)
Freshly ground pepper

1. Peel potatoes and cut enough into ½-inch cubes to measure about 4 cups. Cut unpeeled garlic cloves in half.

2. In large saucepan, combine potatoes, garlic, 1 tablespoon salt, and 6 cups water. Cover and bring to a rolling

boil over high heat. Reduce heat, keeping water at a boil, and continue cooking potatoes 10 to 12 minutes, or until tender. Turn off heat; leave potatoes in water until ready to proceed. Ladle out ⅓ cup of cooking liquid and reserve.

3. Pour off remaining cooking liquid from potatoes; remove garlic, and discard peels. Transfer potatoes and garlic to a food mill or ricer, if using; or you can leave potatoes in saucepan and use a potato masher, in which case you may prefer to remove garlic cloves. Mill, rice, or mash potatoes over medium-size bowl. Add butter and ⅓ cup reserved cooking liquid, and beat potatoes with wooden spoon until fluffy. Add heavy cream, if desired, and beat until blended. Season with salt and pepper to taste.

ADDED TOUCH

These individual jelly tarts are as easy to make as cookies. For variety, you can fill the pastry shells with any type of preserves, jam, or combination of jellies and jams.

Jelly Tarts

2 cups flour
¼ cup sugar
Salt
1 stick butter
1 egg
Prune, quince, apricot, blackberry, or black raspberry preserves

1. In medium-size bowl, combine flour, sugar, and about ¼ teaspoon salt, and stir until blended.

2. With pastry blender or two knives, cut in butter until mixture resembles coarse cornmeal.

3. Separate egg, reserving white for another use. Add yolk and ⅓ cup cold water to flour mixture, and stir until dough can be gathered into a ball. Cover bowl and refrigerate for at least 1 hour.

4. Preheat oven to 375 degrees. Lightly grease baking sheet.

5. On a lightly floured board, roll out chilled pastry to ⅛-inch-thickness. With a knife, cut into 4-inch circles.

6. Turn up outside edge of each circle, forming a narrow rim around tart to contain preserves.

7. Place tarts on sheet and bake 20 minutes, or until lightly golden. Transfer to a rack to cool.

8. Just before serving, place 1 heaping teaspoon preserves in center of each small tart.

Timothy Cass and Robert Van Nood

MENU 1 (Right)
Herb-Stuffed Chicken Breasts with Chèvre-Cream Sauce
Braised Lettuce with Pine Nuts

MENU 2
Poached Trout with Champagne-Tarragon Sauce
Baby Carrots
Sautéed Cucumber Julienne

MENU 3
Braised Endive, Chanterelle, and Bleu d'Auvergne Salad
Sautéed Salmon with Spinach
Fettuccine with Garlic Butter

When Timothy Cass and Robert Van Nood cook French meals, they use only the best of California's seasonal produce. "Quality products don't always find you. You have to look for them," says Timothy Cass. "Our approach to French cooking is classical, reflecting our training," adds Robert Van Nood. "However, we experiment with fresh herbs, grilled meats, and seafood."

In Menu 1, the stuffing for the chicken breasts combines fresh herbs with spinach and watercress, and braised lettuce is served as a side dish. The cooks describe Menu 1 as Norman because of the cream sauce with goat cheese that accompanies the chicken.

Along with experimentation, Robert Van Nood and Timothy Cass value simplicity. Menus 2 and 3 call for an interesting range of ingredients—trout and Champagne, salmon fillets, endive—simply prepared and served. Menu 2 reflects the region of Champagne, where freshwater fish are prized and foods are cooked in the region's famous sparkling wine. In Menu 3, the warm first-course salad with chanterelle mushrooms is reminiscent of Auvergne, where wild mushrooms grow in the forests. The salad also contains a well-known Auvergnac cheese, bleu d'Auvergne.

The chicken breasts are most attractive when sliced and then overlapped on the cream sauce. Garnish the braised lettuce leaves with whole toasted pine nuts and serve a warm loaf of crusty bread to complete the meal.

Herb-Stuffed Chicken Breasts with Chèvre-Cream Sauce
Braised Lettuce with Pine Nuts

Long popular in France, goat cheese, or *chèvre*, has recently caught America's fancy. These tangy cheeses are ideal for a wide range of recipes, including the sauce for these chicken breasts. Goat cheese comes in a variety of shapes and sometimes is coated with ash, pepper, or fragrant herbs. Select a young mild chèvre, such as Montrachet, for this recipe.

WHAT TO DRINK

Many dry white wines would complement this menu. Perhaps the best would be a Graves.

SHOPPING LIST AND STAPLES

2 whole unskinned boneless chicken breasts (about 2 pounds total weight)
4 small heads Bibb lettuce (¾ to 1 pound total weight), or 4 heads Boston lettuce
Small bunch spinach (about ¼ pound)
Large bunch watercress
2 large shallots
Small bunch fresh basil, or 2 teaspoons dried
Small bunch fresh chives
Small bunch fresh mint, or ½ teaspoon dried
Small bunch fresh parsley
Small bunch fresh sage, or 1 teaspoon dried
Small bunch fresh tarragon, or ½ teaspoon dried
½ pint heavy cream
3 tablespoons unsalted butter
¼ pound chèvre, preferably Montrachet, or feta cheese
¼ cup vegetable oil, approximately
2 tablespoons olive oil
3-ounce jar pine nuts
Small bay leaf
Salt
Freshly ground black and white pepper
1 cup dry white wine

UTENSILS

Food processor (optional)
Large skillet
Small skillet
Small heavy-gauge saucepan with cover
17 x 11 x 2-inch roasting pan
Large bowl (if not using food processor)
Small bowl
Salad spinner (optional)
Measuring cups and spoons
Chef's knife
Paring knife
2 wooden spoons
Metal spatula
Rubber spatula
Pastry brush
Wooden toothpicks (optional)

START-TO-FINISH STEPS

1. Follow chicken recipe steps 1 through 4.
2. Follow sauce recipe steps 1 through 4.
3. While sauce is reducing, follow chicken recipe steps 5 and 6.
4. While chicken is cooking, follow lettuce recipe steps 1 and 2.
5. Follow sauce recipe step 5.
6. Follow chicken recipe step 7 and lettuce recipe step 3.
7. While lettuce is cooking, follow sauce recipe step 6 and chicken recipe step 8.
8. Follow lettuce recipe step 4 and serve with chicken and cream sauce.

RECIPES

Herb-Stuffed Chicken Breasts with Chèvre-Cream Sauce

Large bunch watercress
Small bunch spinach
Small bunch fresh parsley
3 fresh basil leaves, or 2 teaspoons dried, crumbled
3 fresh sage leaves, or 1 teaspoon dried, crumbled
3 fresh tarragon leaves, or ½ teaspoon dried, crumbled
1 fresh mint leaf, or ½ teaspoon dried, crumbled
Large shallot
2 tablespoons olive oil
Salt and freshly ground black pepper
2 whole unskinned boneless chicken breasts (about 2 pounds total weight)
¼ cup vegetable oil, approximately
Chèvre-Cream Sauce (see following recipe)

1. Wash greens and fresh herbs, and dry in salad spinner or pat dry with paper towels. Chop enough watercress to

measure 2½ cups, enough spinach to measure 2 cups, and enough parsley to measure ¼ cup. Chop fresh herbs. Peel and coarsely chop shallot.

2. Combine greens and herbs, and chop finely in food processor fitted with metal blade or with chef's knife. Do *not* purée.

3. If using processor, add chopped shallot and olive oil, and process briefly to combine. Or, combine mixture with shallot and olive oil in large bowl. Stuffing mixture should not be smooth. Add salt and pepper to taste; set aside.

4. Preheat oven to 425 degrees. To form pocket for stuffing, gently separate skin from flesh where breastbone was, keeping skin and flesh attached around remaining edges. If necessary, cut out tissue where skin and meat are attached along center of each breast.

5. Fill each pocket with 3 to 4 tablespoons stuffing. With spoon, pat stuffing to form a thin, even layer. Pull skin down around filling, tucking all edges under breast meat. Use wooden toothpicks, if necessary, to contain stuffing and to secure skin to breast.

6. Brush both sides of breasts with vegetable oil, and season with salt and pepper to taste. Place chicken, stuffed side up, in large shallow roasting pan. Bake 12 to 15 minutes, or until skin is brown and crisp, and juices run clear when breasts are pierced with a toothpick.

7. Remove chicken from oven and let cool slightly.

8. Discard toothpicks, if used. Cut each breast in half lengthwise and cut halves into ½-inch-thick slices. Spoon about ¼ cup chèvre-cream sauce onto each dinner plate and top with 4 overlapping slices of chicken.

Chèvre-Cream Sauce

Large shallot
Small bunch fresh chives
1 tablespoon unsalted butter
1 cup dry white wine
Small bay leaf
1 cup heavy cream
Salt and freshly ground white pepper
¼ pound chèvre, preferably Montrachet, or feta cheese

1. Peel and mince shallot. Wash chives, pat dry with paper towels, and mince enough to measure 2 tablespoons.

2. In small heavy-gauge saucepan, melt butter over medium heat. Add shallots and sauté until translucent, about 2 minutes.

3. Add white wine and bay leaf. Over high heat, bring mixture to a boil, stirring constantly, and continue boiling until reduced to about 3 tablespoons, about 7 minutes. Remove bay leaf and discard.

4. Add cream, reduce heat to low, and simmer gently, stirring occasionally, until sauce is reduced to 1 cup, about 20 minutes.

5. Remove pan from heat, season sauce with salt and pepper to taste, and cover to keep warm.

6. When ready to serve, crumble cheese. Working quickly over low heat, stir cheese and chives into sauce, taking care cheese does not melt completely.

Braised Lettuce with Pine Nuts

3 tablespoons pine nuts
4 small heads Bibb lettuce (¾ to 1 pound total weight), or hearts of 4 heads Boston lettuce
2 tablespoons unsalted butter
Salt and freshly ground black pepper

1. In small dry skillet, lightly toast pine nuts over medium heat, shaking pan to prevent scorching, about 3 minutes, or until golden. Set aside.

2. Loosen leaves of Bibb lettuce, rinse in warm water, and refresh in cold water. If using Boston lettuce, remove large outer leaves, loosen inner leaves, and rinse in cool water. Dry lettuce in salad spinner or pat dry with paper towels. Separate leaves.

3. In large skillet, melt butter over low heat. Add a pinch of salt and pepper and lettuce, and cook over low heat, turning occasionally, 2 to 3 minutes, or just until warm.

4. Divide lettuce leaves among 4 dinner plates and top with pine nuts.

ADDED TOUCH

For the best results, use just-ripe peaches that will not become pulpy during cooking, or, if unavailable, substitute Bartlett pears.

Poached Peaches in Wine Sauce

4 mint sprigs for garnish (optional)
4 small to medium-size freestone peaches
3 cups dry white wine
½ cup plus 1 teaspoon peach brandy or pear brandy, if using pears
1½ cups sugar
½ teaspoon cornstarch
1 pint vanilla ice cream (optional)

1. If using mint sprigs for garnish, wash and pat dry with paper towels; set aside.

2. Bring 2 quarts water to a boil in medium-size saucepan. With slotted spoon, immerse each peach in boiling water 30 seconds, and then plunge into cold water so skin will peel off easily. With paring knife, peel, halve, and pit peaches. If using pears, peel, halve, and core them. Discard liquid and rinse saucepan.

3. In same pan, combine wine, ½ cup brandy, and sugar in pan, and bring to a boil over medium-high heat. Add fruit, reduce heat so that liquid simmers, and poach fruit just until soft, about 7 minutes. With slotted spoon, transfer fruit to medium-size bowl and keep warm. Reserve 1 cup poaching liquid; discard remainder.

4. In small bowl, blend cornstarch and remaining brandy. In small saucepan, bring reserved poaching liquid to a boil over medium-high heat. Add cornstarch mixture, reduce heat, and simmer gently, stirring constantly, 1 minute, or until sauce thickens.

5. Divide peaches or pears among dessert plates and pour about ¼ cup sauce over each serving. Top with 1 scoop vanilla ice cream and garnish with mint sprigs, if desired.

Poached Trout in Tarragon-Cream Sauce
Baby Carrots
Sautéed Cucumber Julienne

The main course of poached trout in cream sauce is garnished with a sprig of fresh tarragon. Served with sautéed baby carrots and cucumber julienne, this is an impressive meal for family or company.

Use fresh brook or rainbow trout for this dish. Ask your fish dealer to pan dress each fish. Leave the skin intact to help the fish retain its shape while poaching. If you wish, remove it before serving.

The cooks suggest using a mandoline, if you have one, to prepare the cucumber julienne. The basic mandoline is a simple set of blades fixed to a wooden frame. To use it, move the cucumber rhythmically across the blades, pushing with the heel of your hand.

WHAT TO DRINK

White Burgundy always goes well with trout. Try a Mersault, a Puligny-Montrachet, or a California Chardonnay.

SHOPPING LIST AND STAPLES

4 butterflied brook or rainbow trout (each 8 to 10 ounces), with skins intact
¾ pound baby carrots (about 20)
2 small cucumbers
Small shallot
Small bunch fresh dill, or 1 teaspoon dried
Small bunch fresh mint, or ¼ teaspoon dried (optional)
Small bunch fresh tarragon, or 2 teaspoons dried
½ pint heavy cream
4½ tablespoons unsalted butter
1 bay leaf
Salt
Freshly ground black and white pepper
3 cups dry Champagne or other dry white wine

UTENSILS

Large sauté pan or deep skillet with cover
2 medium-size skillets
Medium-size saucepan
2 small saucepans, one with cover
Heatproof platter
Medium-size bowl
Colander
Measuring cups and spoons
Chef's knife
Paring knife
Slotted spoon
2 large spatulas
Mandoline (optional)
Vegetable peeler (optional)

1. Follow carrots recipe steps 1 and 2.
2. While carrots are cooking, follow cucumber recipe steps 1 and 2, and trout recipe step 1.
3. Follow carrots recipe step 3 and trout recipe steps 2 through 9.
4. While sauce is simmering, follow carrots recipe steps 4 and 5.
5. Follow trout recipe step 10.
6. Follow cucumber recipe steps 3 and 4, trout recipe step 11, and serve with carrots.

RECIPES

Poached Trout in Tarragon-Cream Sauce

4 butterflied brook or rainbow trout (each 8 to 10 ounces), with skins intact
Salt and freshly ground black pepper
Small bunch fresh tarragon, or 2 teaspoons dried
Small shallot
1 tablespoon unsalted butter
3 cups dry Champagne or other dry white wine
1 bay leaf
1 cup heavy cream

1. Preheat oven to 200 degrees. Place heatproof platter and 4 dinner plates in oven to warm. Wipe fish with damp paper towels. Season inside of body cavity with salt and pepper to taste.
2. Wash fresh tarragon, if using, and pat dry with paper towels. Chop enough tarragon leaves to measure 1 tablespoon for sauce and set aside; reserve 4 sprigs for garnish, if desired. Peel and chop shallot.
3. In large sauté pan or deep skillet, melt butter over medium heat. Add shallot and sauté just until translucent, 2 to 3 minutes.
4. Add Champagne and bay leaf to skillet and bring mixture to a boil.
5. Carefully place trout in pan and reduce heat to low. Cover pan and gently simmer fish until firm, about 5 minutes.
6. Using 2 large spatulas, transfer trout to warmed heatproof platter, cover loosely with foil, and place in oven to keep warm.
7. Remove bay leaf from poaching liquid and discard. Measure half of liquid into small saucepan and discard remainder. Over medium heat, bring liquid to a boil and reduce until it has consistency of molasses, about 7 minutes.
8. While sauce is reducing, if desired, remove skin from trout using paring knife.
9. Transfer reduced liquid to another small saucepan. Add cream, bring to a boil over medium heat, and simmer gently until slightly thickened, about 5 minutes.
10. Add chopped or dried tarragon to sauce, cover pan, and remove from heat.
11. Transfer trout to warm dinner plates. Pour sauce over

and around each trout and garnish with tarragon sprigs, if using.

Baby Carrots

¾ pound baby carrots (about 20)
Small bunch fresh dill, or 1 teaspoon dried
Salt
2 tablespoons unsalted butter
Freshly ground black pepper

1. With chef's knife, remove leafy tops, if any, from carrots, and scrape carrots with a vegetable peeler. If using fresh dill, wash, pat dry with paper towels, and chop enough to measure 1 tablespoon.
2. In medium-size saucepan, bring 2 cups water and ½ teaspoon salt to a boil over high heat. Add carrots, return to a boil, and cook until barely tender when pierced with paring knife, about 10 minutes.
3. With slotted spoon, transfer carrots to medium-size bowl and rinse under cold running water. Fill bowl with enough cold water to cover carrots and set aside.
4. In medium-size skillet, melt butter over medium heat. Do not let butter brown. Quickly drain carrots in colander and pat dry with paper towels. Add carrots, dill, and salt and pepper to taste to melted butter, and toss carrots until evenly coated and just heated through, about 3 minutes.
5. Transfer carrots to heatproof bowl and keep warm in 200-degree oven.

Sautéed Cucumber Julienne

2 small cucumbers
1½ tablespoons unsalted butter
Salt and freshly ground white pepper

1. Peel cucumbers; trim ends and discard. With chef's knife, halve cucumbers lengthwise. Scoop out seeds with teaspoon, if necessary.
2. Cut cucumber halves crosswise into 3-inch lengths. With mandoline or chef's knife, slice lengthwise into ¼-inch-thick strips. Set aside.
3. In medium-size skillet, melt butter over low heat. Season cucumbers with salt and pepper to taste. Add cucumbers to skillet, and cook, tossing in butter until just warm, about 3 minutes.
4. With slotted spoon, transfer cucumbers to dinner plates.

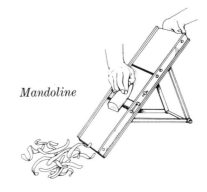

Mandoline

Braised Endive, Chanterelle, and Bleu d'Auvergne Salad
Sautéed Salmon with Spinach
Fettuccine with Garlic Butter

The warm salad is a medley of slightly bitter chicory (curly endive), Belgian endive, chanterelle mushrooms, and pungent bleu d'Auvergne cheese. This cow's milk cheese with blue veins is available at gourmet shops. Refrigerated in plastic wrap, it will keep two to three weeks. As a substitute, use a domestic or imported blue cheese, such as Oregon or Danish blue.

For the main course, buy salmon fillets with the skins removed. Before cooking, check for bones by running your fingers against the grain of the flesh. Any tiny bones that remain can be removed easily with tweezers. The herb butter for the salmon can be made with any combination of fresh seasonal herbs—freeze leftover herb purée for another use.

WHAT TO DRINK

A top-quality Sancerre or a Pouilly-Fumé from the northern Loire Valley would be a good selection here.

SHOPPING LIST AND STAPLES

Four ½- to 1-inch-thick salmon fillets (1¾ to 2 pounds total weight)
¼ pound chanterelles, or other fresh mushrooms

For this elegant Auvergnac-style supper, place each salmon fillet on a bed of spinach and top with herb butter. Offer the fettuccine in light garlic sauce and a warm salad of endive, mushrooms, and blue cheese as accompaniments.

2 to 3 medium-size bunches spinach (about 1½ pounds total weight)
2 small heads Belgian endive
Small head chicory (curly endive)
Small bunch watercress
Small bunch parsley
Small bunch fresh chives, or 1 teaspoon freeze-dried
Small bunch fresh basil, or 1 teaspoon dried
Small bunch fresh dill, or 1 teaspoon dried
Small bunch fresh mint, or 1 teaspoon dried
Small bunch fresh tarragon, or 1 teaspoon dried
1 clove garlic
2 sticks lightly salted butter
1 stick unsalted butter
¼ pound bleu d'Auvergne or other blue cheese
½ pound fettuccine, preferably fresh, or dried
½ cup walnut oil
2 tablespoons olive oil
2 tablespoons vegetable oil
2 tablespoons raspberry vinegar
4-ounce can walnut pieces
¼ cup flour, approximately
Salt
Freshly ground black pepper
Freshly ground white pepper
3 tablespoons brandy

UTENSILS

Food processor or blender
Large heavy-gauge skillet
Medium-size skillet
Large saucepan
Large sauté pan
Medium-size sauté pan
Medium-size bowl
Small bowl
Colander
Salad spinner (optional)
Measuring cups and spoons
Chef's knife
2 wooden spoons
Slotted spoon
Metal spatula
Rubber spatula
Small whisk

START-TO-FINISH STEPS

1. Follow herb butter recipe steps 1 through 3.
2. Follow salad recipe steps 1 through 4.
3. Follow salmon recipe steps 1 through 6 and salad recipe step 5.

4. Turn fillets, follow salmon recipe step 7, and fettuccine recipe step 1.

5. Follow salmon recipe step 8 and salad recipe step 6.

6. Follow fettuccine recipe step 2.

7. While fettuccine is cooking, follow salad recipe steps 7 and 8.

8. Follow salmon recipe step 9, fettuccine recipe steps 3 and 4, and serve with salad.

RECIPES

Braised Endive, Chanterelle, and Bleu d'Auvergne Salad

4-ounce can walnut pieces
Small head chicory
2 small heads Belgian endive
¼ pound chanterelles or other fresh mushrooms
2 tablespoons raspberry vinegar
6 tablespoons walnut oil
Salt
Freshly ground black pepper
4 tablespoons lightly salted butter
2 tablespoons brandy
¼ pound bleu d'Auvergne cheese

1. Coarsely chop enough walnut pieces to measure ¼ cup; set aside.

2. Wash chicory and dry in salad spinner or pat dry. Break enough into bite-size pieces to measure about 2 cups. Trim bases of Belgian endive; loosen and separate into spears. Rinse chanterelles under cold water and pat dry.

3. For vinaigrette, pour vinegar into small bowl. Add walnut oil in a slow, steady stream, whisking vigorously until blended. Season with salt and pepper to taste; set aside.

4. Place chicory in medium-size bowl. Add walnuts and vinaigrette to taste, and toss until evenly coated. Divide among 4 salad bowls.

5. In medium-size skillet, melt 2 tablespoons butter over medium heat. Add 4 to 6 endive spears per person and toss until warm, 1 to 2 minutes. Divide among salad bowls.

6. In same skillet, melt remaining butter over medium heat. Add chanterelles and sauté until browned, about 3 minutes. Spoon off excess butter, remove pan from heat, and add brandy. Averting your face, carefully ignite brandy with match. When flames subside, spoon mushrooms and their liquid over salads.

7. Crumble cheese and sprinkle over salads.

8. Place salad bowls in oven briefly to warm cheese.

Sautéed Salmon with Spinach

2 to 3 bunches fresh spinach (about 1½ pounds total weight)
Four ½- to 1-inch-thick salmon fillets (1¾ to 2 pounds total weight)
Salt and freshly ground white pepper
¼ cup flour, approximately
2 tablespoons vegetable oil
3 tablespoons lightly salted butter
Herb Butter (see following recipe)

1. Preheat oven to 200 degrees.

2. Wash spinach and dry in salad spinner or pat dry with paper towels. Remove stems and discard. Set aside.

3. Wipe salmon fillets with damp paper towels. Season with salt and pepper to taste.

4. Place flour on sheet of waxed paper. Lightly dredge each fillet in flour; gently shake off excess.

5. Place 4 dinner plates in oven to warm.

6. In large heavy-gauge skillet, heat oil over medium-high heat. Add fillets and sauté 4 minutes, or until golden. Reduce heat to low, turn fillets carefully with spatula, and cook another 4 to 6 minutes, or until fish is firm.

7. Meanwhile, melt butter in large sauté pan over medium heat. Add spinach and cook, tossing, 3 to 4 minutes, or just until wilted. Season with salt and pepper to taste.

8. Divide spinach among warm dinner plates, forming beds for salmon. Place 1 fillet in each bed and top and return to oven until ready to serve.

9. Just before serving, remove salmon from oven and top each serving with a generous spoonful of herb butter.

Herb Butter

¼ cup watercress leaves
½ cup parsley sprigs
2 fresh basil leaves, or ½ teaspoon dried
4 fresh dill sprigs, or 1 teaspoon dried
3 fresh mint leaves, or 1 teaspoon dried
1 tablespoon chopped fresh tarragon, or 1 teaspoon dried
1 tablespoon snipped fresh chives, or 1 teaspoon freeze-dried
2 tablespoons olive oil
1 stick unsalted butter, softened

1 tablespoon brandy
Salt
Freshly ground black pepper

1. Wash watercress, parsley, and fresh herbs, if using. Pat dry with paper towels. Chop enough tarragon and chives to measure 1 tablespoon each.
2. In food processor fitted with metal blade or in blender, combine watercress, parsley, and fresh or dried herbs. Purée, adding olive oil in a slow, steady stream. Stop when oil is blended into greens, scrape down sides of bowl with rubber spatula, and process to a fine purée.
3. In small mixing bowl, combine softened butter with herb purée to taste; freeze remaining purée for another use. Stir in brandy and season with salt and pepper to taste. Cover and refrigerate.

Fettuccine with Garlic Butter

2 teaspoons salt
1 clove garlic
½ pound fettuccine, preferably fresh, or dried
2 tablespoons lightly salted butter
Freshly ground white pepper (optional)

1. In large saucepan, bring 2 quarts water and 2 teaspoons salt to a boil. Peel and chop garlic; set aside.
2. Stir fettuccine into boiling water. It should not cook more than 2 to 3 minutes if using fresh fettuccine, or 5 to 7 minutes if using dried.
3. Drain fettuccine in colander.
4. In medium-size sauté pan, melt butter over medium heat. Add garlic and fettuccine to pan, and toss until warmed through, 2 to 3 minutes. Season with pepper to taste, if using, and divide evenly among dinner plates.

ADDED TOUCH

For delicate crêpes, prepare the batter an hour or more ahead so that the flour particles can expand.

Crêpes Calvados

Crêpes:
3 tablespoons unsalted butter, approximately
1 large or 2 small eggs
⅓ cup flour
1½ teaspoons sugar
2 tablespoons vegetable oil
½ cup milk

Apple filling:
2 medium-size Granny Smith or other tart apples
  (about 1 pound total weight)
2 tablespoons unsalted butter
2 tablespoons sugar
½ cup Calvados or other apple brandy
1 teaspoon freshly squeezed lemon juice
1 teaspoon cornstarch
Pinch of cinnamon

Confectioners' sugar
1 cup heavy cream for garnish, chilled

1. For crêpes, melt butter in small pan over low heat. In small bowl, beat 1 large egg or 2 small eggs with fork.
2. In medium-size mixing bowl, combine flour and sugar. Add egg, vegetable oil, 1½ tablespoons of the butter, and milk. With wire whisk or electric mixer, beat batter until smooth. Set aside, preferably for 1 hour.
3. If using cream, place large bowl and beaters in freezer to chill.
4. For filling, peel, core, and dice enough apples to measure 3 cups. In medium-size skillet, heat butter over medium heat until sizzling. Add apples and sugar, and cook, stirring occasionally, until apples are slightly caramelized, about 8 minutes. Turn off heat.
5. Remove pan from heat and add Calvados. Averting your face, hold a match just above skillet and ignite. Shake pan gently until flames subside.
6. Blend lemon juice, cornstarch, and cinnamon, with 1 tablespoon water. Stir into apple mixture in skillet; set aside.
7. If using cream, beat in chilled bowl with chilled beaters until standing in soft peaks.
8. Set crêpe pan or small nonstick skillet with sloping sides over medium heat until hot. Brush bottom of pan with 1 teaspoon melted butter. Pour in 3 tablespoons batter. Tilt and turn pan to coat bottom evenly. Return pan to heat and cook crêpe until somewhat set and edges are lightly colored. With tongs or spatula, turn crêpe and cook another 30 seconds. Transfer crêpe to waxed-paper-lined platter. Cover crêpe with another sheet of waxed paper. Repeat with remaining batter to make three more crêpes.
9. Return apple mixture to medium-high heat and cook, stirring constantly, until thickened, about 30 seconds.
10. Top each crêpe with 3 to 4 tablespoonfuls of filling, roll up, and sprinkle with confectioners' sugar. Serve garnished with whipped cream, if desired.

Karen Hubert and Len Allison

P artners Len Allison and Karen Hubert represent a new breed of free-spirited American cook. "We create meals from different ethnic cultures," says Len Allison, "but our recipes are really interpretations of the classics. We enjoy being imaginative."

One such interpretation is their Menu 1, which features a meal influenced by Basque cuisine. The Basques, great fishermen, often sauce their fish with tomatoes and peppers. Here, the snapper—pan-browned almost to the point of blackening—is served with a thickened tomato marinade. Sweet corn is an unlikely vegetable for a French menu, but maize has been grown in the Basque country since its importation from America in the sixteenth century, and cornmeal is used in many traditional cakes and breads of the region. The cooks' interpretation is a side dish of individual corn puddings.

Menu 2 is a more sophisticated *nouvelle-cuisine* style meal that a Parisian cook might assemble. Veal sweetbreads are paired with baby vegetables and served with sweet rice (actually, a combination of Japanese sweet rice and regular long-grain rice) flavored with lemon grass, a popular Asian seasoning.

Menu 3 calls for some Alsatian favorites: pork with mushrooms, red cabbage, and noodles. The cooks transform the dish with two Oriental seasonings: soy sauce and *mirin*, a Japanese rice wine.

Breaded green tomato slices and red snapper fillets topped with a rich tomato sauce comprise the entrée for this fall or winter meal. Provide guests with individual ramekins of creamy corn pudding garnished with sliced scallions and add a napkin-lined basket of French bread.

Pan-Blackened Red Snapper
Corn Pudding
Fried Green Tomatoes

The pan-blackened red snapper fillets have a crisp skin yet are moist inside. To brown the fish properly, the cooks recommend using a cast-iron skillet because it absorbs heat uniformly and then retains it. The pale yellow clarified butter in which you brown the fish is melted butter with the milk solids removed (see page 10 for instructions). Use the clarified butter merely to coat the surface of the skillet: The fish will brown—almost blacken—from the intense heat of the skillet. If you wish an even darker crust on the fish, transfer the fillets to a broiler pan and broil for a few seconds after sautéing.

Green tomatoes, which are firm but not overly juicy, are ideal for frying. The bread-crumb coating keeps the slices intact, seals in moisture, and forms a crisp crust. Two or three thick slices per person are ample. You can substitute firm, ripe tomatoes. Or, in the absence of perfect tomatoes, you can substitute a large zucchini and reduce the cooking time.

WHAT TO DRINK

To stand up to the distinctive flavors of these recipes, a substantial white wine is needed. A white Châteauneuf-du-Pape or Crozes-Hermitages would provide the appropriate south-of-France note. Alternatively, a crisp California Sauvignon Blanc would also taste fine.

SHOPPING LIST AND STAPLES

Four ⅓- to ½-inch-thick fillets of red snapper, unskinned (1½ to 2 pounds total weight)
2 large ripe, red tomatoes (about 1¼ pounds total weight)
3 medium-size green tomatoes (about ¾ pound total weight)
1 ear fresh corn, or 10-ounce package frozen kernels
Small bunch chives
Small bunch scallions
2 limes
3 eggs
½ pint half-and-half
2 sticks unsalted butter, approximately
¾ cup beef stock, preferably homemade, or 13½-ounce can
½ cup all-purpose flour, approximately
1 teaspoon cornstarch
½ cup unseasoned, fine, dry bread crumbs

½ teaspoon anise seed
¼ teaspoon Cayenne pepper
Salt
Freshly ground pepper
½ cup dry white wine

UTENSILS

2 large cast-iron skillets, or 2 medium-size plus 1 large skillet
Medium-size saucepan
Small heavy-gauge saucepan or butter warmer
8 x 8-inch baking pan
Four 4-ounce ramekins
Medium-size nonaluminum bowl
Medium-size mixing bowl
Small shallow bowl
Measuring cups and spoons
Chef's knife
Paring knife
Wooden spoon
Spatula
Ladle
Juicer (optional)
Whisk
Mortar and pestle

START-TO-FINISH STEPS

Fifteen minutes ahead: Clarify butter (see page 10) for fish recipe.

1. Wash green tomatoes and pat dry; slice crosswise into ¼-inch rounds. Peel, seed, and chop red tomatoes for fish recipe. Rinse chives and scallions, and pat dry. Mince chives for fish recipe; trim and chop scallions for corn recipe.
2. Follow fish recipe step 1.
3. Follow corn pudding recipe steps 1 through 6 and green tomato recipe steps 1 through 3.
4. Follow fish recipe steps 2 through 5.
5. Check corn puddings for doneness. If done, reduce oven temperature to 200 degrees, leaving oven door ajar a few moments to hasten temperature reduction.
6. Follow green tomato recipe steps 4 and 5.
7. Follow fish recipe steps 6 and 7, corn pudding recipe step 7, and serve with green tomatoes.

Pan-Blackened Red Snapper

2 limes
2 cups peeled, seeded, and coarsely chopped ripe, red
  tomatoes
½ cup dry white wine
Four ⅓- to ½-inch-thick fillets of red snapper, unskinned
Salt and freshly ground pepper
¾ cup beef stock
3 tablespoons minced chives
4 tablespoons clarified unsalted butter, plus 4 tablespoons
  unclarified, chilled

1. Juice enough limes to measure ¼ cup. Combine lime juice with tomatoes and wine in medium-size non-aluminum bowl. Place fish fillets, flesh side down, in marinade. Let stand at room temperature 20 to 30 minutes.
2. Remove fish from marinade and pat dry with paper towels. Sprinkle each fillet with salt and pepper. Reserve marinade.
3. For sauce, transfer marinade to medium-size saucepan and bring to a boil over medium-high heat. Continue boiling about 10 minutes, or until reduced by half.
4. Stir in stock and 2 tablespoons minced chives, and boil another 15 minutes, or until syrupy and reduced to 1 cup.
5. Reduce heat to low. Stir in chilled butter, 1 tablespoon at a time (sauce will thicken as butter melts). Add salt and pepper to taste. Keep warm over very low heat.
6. Set large cast-iron skillet or 2 medium-size skillets over high heat until smoking. Pour in clarified butter. Carefully place fillets, flesh side down, in skillet and sauté several minutes over high heat. Check edges of fillets for color; when fish is very brown, almost black, turn and cook other side until well browned. Total cooking time is 6 to 8 minutes, depending on thickness of fillets.
7. Divide fillets among individual plates, top with sauce, and sprinkle with remaining 1 tablespoon chives.

Corn Pudding

2 tablespoons unsalted butter
1 ear fresh corn, or ½ cup frozen kernels
½ teaspoon anise seed
2 eggs
1 cup half-and-half
1 tablespoon chopped scallion, green part only, plus
  2 tablespoons for garnish (optional)

1 teaspoon cornstarch
½ teaspoon salt
¼ teaspoon Cayenne pepper
Freshly ground pepper

1. Adjust rack to center of oven. Preheat oven to 350 degrees.
2. In small heavy-gauge saucepan or butter warmer, melt butter over low heat. Set aside to cool.
3. Meanwhile, if using fresh corn, husk; hull enough kernels to measure ½ cup. With mortar and pestle, crush anise seed to fine texture.
4. Beat eggs in medium-size mixing bowl. Add melted butter, half-and-half, corn, cornstarch, 1 tablespoon scallion, the anise seed, salt, Cayenne, and pepper to taste, and stir until combined.
5. Butter four 4-ounce ramekins. Divide mixture among them.
6. Place ramekins in baking pan and fill with lukewarm water to a depth of 1 inch. Bake 20 to 25 minutes, or until centers of puddings are firm to touch.
7. Set ramekins on small plates and serve garnished with chopped scallion, if desired.

Fried Green Tomatoes

3 medium-size green tomatoes, sliced
Salt
Freshly ground pepper
1 egg
½ cup all-purpose flour, approximately
½ cup unseasoned, fine, dry bread crumbs,
  approximately
¼ cup unsalted butter

1. Sprinkle both sides of tomato slices with salt and pepper.
2. Beat egg with 1 tablespoon water in small shallow bowl. Place flour and bread crumbs on separate sheets of waxed paper.
3. Dredge tomato slices with flour, dip into egg mixture (let excess drip off), then dredge with bread crumbs. Place in single layer on waxed paper to dry for several minutes, or until ready to proceed.
4. In large skillet, melt butter over medium-high heat. When foam subsides, add tomato slices and sauté about 3 minutes per side, or until brown.
5. Divide among individual dinner plates and keep warm in 200-degree oven until ready to serve.

Sweetbreads with Baby Vegetables in Lemon-Cream Sauce
Sweet Rice

For a visually impressive meal, carefully arrange the sautéed sweetbreads and the molded sweet rice on each dinner plate. Then ladle the baby vegetables in the tangy lemon sauce over the sweetbreads just before serving.

S weetbreads, the thymus glands of calves, are a delicacy stocked by the meat department of many supermarkets. Rinse sweetbreads thoroughly in cold water before cooking. Poach them first to firm their texture, peel off the external membrane, then sauté them.

Japanese sweet, or glutinous, rice is a short-grained, starchy rice popular in many Asian cuisines. The rice should be thoroughly rinsed and drained before cooking. Combining sweet rice with a standard long-grain rice produces a dish with sturdier texture. Sweet rice may be purchased at Oriental groceries or specialty food shops.

Fresh lemon grass, an aromatic Asian ingredient used here to flavor the rice, has a tough, bulbous stalk with a strong lemony taste. Bruise the stalks with the flat of a chef's knife to release the lemon flavor. Fresh stalks keep for several months in the refrigerator. If you cannot get fresh lemon grass, try dried, which you must soak for two hours before use. Twelve strips of dried lemon grass equal one fresh stalk. Both fresh and dried lemon grass are sold at Oriental groceries.

WHAT TO DRINK

The sweetbreads demand a rich, full-bodied white wine, such as a good California Chardonnay or a top-flight (*grand cru*) Chablis.

SHOPPING LIST AND STAPLES

1½ pounds veal sweetbreads
Medium-size onion
8 baby Belgian carrots (about ½ pound total weight)
8 baby yellow squash (about ½ pound total weight)
¼ pound sugar snap peas
Small lemon, plus one additional if not using lemon grass
2-inch piece of lemon grass, if available
1 pint milk
½ pint heavy cream
6 tablespoons unsalted butter
2¾ cups chicken stock, preferably homemade
    (see page 11), or canned
½ pound Japanese sweet rice
½ pound long-grain rice
½ cup all-purpose flour
2 whole cloves
Salt and freshly ground pepper
¼ cup dry white wine

UTENSILS

Medium-size skillet with cover
Large saucepan
2 medium-size saucepans, one heavy-gauge with cover
   and one nonaluminum
Small heavy-gauge saucepan or butter warmer
Four 4-ounce ramekins
Large flat plate
Colander
Collapsible vegetable steamer
Measuring cups and spoons
Chef's knife
Paring knife
Wooden spoon
Spatula
Slotted spatula
Ladle

START-TO-FINISH STEPS

Fifteen minutes ahead: Clarify 4 tablespoons butter (see page 10) for sweetbreads recipe.

1. Follow sweetbreads recipe steps 1 through 3.
2. Follow rice recipe steps 1 through 4.
3. While rice is cooking, follow sauce recipe steps 1 through 3.
4. Follow sweetbreads recipe step 4.
5. Follow rice recipe step 5 and turn off heat under sauce.
6. Follow sweetbreads recipe steps 5 and 6.
7. Follow rice recipe step 6, sweetbreads recipe step 7, and serve.

RECIPES

Sweetbreads with Baby Vegetables in Lemon-Cream Sauce

Medium-size onion
2 cloves
1½ pounds veal sweetbreads
1 cup milk
8 baby Belgian carrots
8 baby yellow squash
1 cup sugar snap peas
Salt and freshly ground pepper
½ cup all-purpose flour
4 tablespoons clarified unsalted butter (see page 10), plus
   2 tablespoons unclarified
Lemon-Cream Sauce (see following recipe)

1. Peel onion and stick with cloves. Cut sweetbreads into 4 equal sections.
2. In large saucepan, combine onion, milk, and water to cover, and bring to a boil over high heat. Reduce heat and simmer 10 minutes. Turn off heat and allow to rest.
3. Meanwhile, prepare vegetables: Trim, wash, and pat dry with paper towels. In saucepan fitted with collapsible steamer, steam vegetables separately until barely tender: carrots for 8 minutes; squash, 6 minutes; and sugar snap peas, 4 minutes. As they are done, transfer vegetables to colander and refresh under cold running water; set aside.
4. Line plate with paper towels. Place flour on sheet of waxed paper. Transfer sweetbreads to paper-towel-lined plate; pat dry. Season sweetbreads with salt and pepper, and dredge in flour, gently shaking off excess.
5. Combine clarified butter with remaining butter in medium-size skillet over medium-high heat. When foaming subsides, add sweetbreads. Reduce heat to medium, cover, and cook about 8 minutes, or until lightly browned. Turn sweetbreads and brown other side.
6. Meanwhile, add steamed vegetables to Lemon-Cream Sauce and reheat briefly over low heat, if necessary.
7. Slice sweetbreads thinly and divide among individual plates. Spoon vegetables and sauce over sweetbreads.

Lemon-Cream Sauce

Small lemon
¼ cup dry white wine
¾ cup chicken stock
⅓ cup heavy cream
Salt and freshly ground pepper

1. Peel lemon, avoiding white pith, and mince enough peel to measure 1 teaspoon; squeeze 2 tablespoons juice.
2. Combine peel, juice, and wine in medium-size nonaluminum saucepan. Bring to a boil over high heat and continue to boil 1 minute, until slightly reduced. Remove pan from heat.
3. Stir in stock, heavy cream, and salt and pepper to taste. Return to low heat and simmer, stirring frequently, 20 minutes, or until thick.

Sweet Rice

2-inch piece lemon grass, or small lemon
2 cups chicken stock
1 cup milk
¾ teaspoon salt
1 cup Japanese sweet rice
1 cup long-grain rice

1. If not using lemon grass, cut several thin strips of lemon zest.
2. In medium-size saucepan used for vegetables, combine stock, milk, salt, and 1 cup water, and bring to a boil over high heat.
3. Add lemon grass or zest and stir in both rices. Reduce heat to low and simmer, uncovered, 10 minutes. Cover pan and cook another 10 minutes. Rice will be sticky and will have absorbed all liquid. Reserve lemon grass or peel for garnish, if desired.
4. Preheat oven to 200 degrees.
5. Butter four 4-ounce ramekins. Pack rice into ramekins, cover with foil, and keep warm in 200-degree oven.
6. When ready to serve, unmold rice onto dinner plates and garnish with lemon grass or peel, if desired.

Scallops of Pork with Mushrooms
Braised Red Cabbage
Alsatian Noodles

Pork scallops with mushrooms, red cabbage, and noodles—with mugs of dark beer—make a filling Alsatian meal.

Scallops of pork, braised red cabbage, and noodles comprise an excellent cold-weather family dinner. Pork scallops are thick, tender, boneless cutlets from the center loin of pork. The recipe for the sauce calls for fresh wild mushrooms. Try to find golden oak, chanterelles, shiitake, or magutake; if not available, substitute domestic white-capped mushrooms. For this recipe use Japanese-style soy sauce, which is lighter in consistency—though not in color—than the Chinese sauces, which may contain molasses and are usually saltier as well. Look for the syrupy-sweet *mirin* in specialty food shops and well-stocked supermarkets. If you cannot find it, substitute sweet sherry. Freshly made noodles are widely available, but if you must substitute dried, follow package directions.

WHAT TO DRINK

Good dark beer is a fitting accompaniment to this Alsatian meal. Just as appropriate would be a good Alsatian white wine: Sylvaner, Pinot Blanc, or Gewürztraminer.

SHOPPING LIST AND STAPLES

8 pork scallops, pounded to ¼-inch thickness (about 1¼ pounds total weight)
¼ pound fresh wild mushrooms
Medium-size head red cabbage
Medium-size red onion
Small bunch parsley or chives
2 large tart apples (about 1 pound total weight)
Small lemon
1 stick plus 1 tablespoon unsalted butter, approximately
¼ pound fresh egg noodles
2 cups chicken stock, preferably homemade (see page 11), or canned
¼ cup peanut oil, approximately
½ cup cider vinegar
1 tablespoon soy sauce
⅓ cup all-purpose flour, approximately
½ cup light brown sugar
3 whole cloves
2 whole allspice, or 1 teaspoon ground
1 bay leaf
Freshly grated nutmeg
Salt and freshly ground pepper
¾ to 1¼ cups dry red wine
1 tablespoon mirin or sweet sherry

UTENSILS

Food processor (optional)
Stock pot
Large skillet
Large heavy-gauge saucepan with cover
Colander
Measuring cups and spoons
Chef's knife
Paring knife
Grater (if not using processor)
Apple corer (optional)

START-TO-FINISH STEPS

1. Follow cabbage recipe steps 1 and 2, and pork recipe step 1.
2. Follow cabbage recipe step 3.
3. Follow pork recipe steps 2 through 6 and noodles recipe step 1.
4. Follow pork recipe step 7 and noodles recipe steps 2 through 4.
5. Follow pork recipe step 8 and cabbage recipe step 4.
6. Follow noodles recipe step 5, pork recipe step 9, and serve with cabbage.

RECIPES

Scallops of Pork with Mushrooms

¼ pound fresh wild mushrooms
Small lemon
⅓ cup all-purpose flour, approximately
Salt and freshly ground pepper
8 pork scallops, pounded to ¼-inch thickness (about 1¼ pounds total weight)
¼ cup peanut oil, approximately
2 tablespoons unsalted butter, approximately
¼ cup dry red wine
2 cups chicken stock
1 tablespoon soy sauce
1 tablespoon mirin or sweet sherry

1. Preheat oven to 200 degrees.
2. Wipe mushrooms with damp paper towels. Thinly slice enough mushrooms to measure 2 cups. Squeeze enough lemon to measure 1 tablespoon juice. Set aside.
3. Place heatproof platter and 4 dinner plates in oven to warm.

4. Place flour on sheet of waxed paper. Salt and pepper both sides of scallops, then dredge lightly in flour, shaking gently to remove excess.

5. Combine oil and 1 tablespoon butter in large skillet over high heat. When foam subsides, add 4 scallops and sauté quickly, 2 to 3 minutes per side, or until browned. Transfer to warm platter as soon as each is brown—do not overcook. Repeat with remaining 4 scallops, adding more oil and butter to skillet, if necessary.

6. Pour off excess oil and return skillet to heat. Add wine and bring to a boil over high heat. Cook until slightly reduced, about 3 minutes.

7. Add chicken stock, soy sauce, mirin, and lemon juice, and return to a boil. Stir in mushrooms, reduce heat to low, and simmer, stirring occasionally, 10 to 15 minutes, or until liquid is reduced by half.

8. Adjust seasonings. Stir in remaining tablespoon butter, return scallops to sauce, and reheat briefly, turning once to coat.

9. Divide scallops among warm dinner plates and top with sauce.

Braised Red Cabbage

Medium-size red onion
2 large tart apples (about 1 pound total weight)
Medium-size head red cabbage
2 tablespoons unsalted butter
½ cup light brown sugar
3 whole cloves
2 whole allspice, or 1 teaspoon ground
1 bay leaf
1 teaspoon salt
½ cup cider vinegar
½ to 1 cup dry red wine

1. Peel onions and slice thinly with chef's knife or with food processor fitted with slicing blade. Rinse apples and pat dry. Halve, core, and slice similarly. Remove tough or blemished outer leaves of cabbage. Shred finely on coarse side of hand-held grater or, if using processor, change to shredding blade and process.

2. In large heavy-gauge saucepan, melt butter over medium heat. Add onion and sauté 3 to 4 minutes, until wilted but not browned.

3. Add apples, cabbage, sugar, cloves, allspice, bay leaf, salt, vinegar, and enough wine to moisten thoroughly, and bring to a boil over high heat. Reduce heat to low, cover, and simmer, stirring occasionally, 30 to 35 minutes, or until tender.

4. Before serving, drain off some liquid, if necessary, and remove cloves and bay leaf.

Alsatian Noodles

Salt
Small bunch parsley or chives
½ pound fresh egg noodles
1 tablespoon unsalted butter
Freshly ground pepper
Freshly grated nutmeg

1. Bring 3 quarts salted water to a boil in stockpot over high heat.

2. While water is heating, wash parsley or chives and pat dry with paper towels; mince enough to measure ¼ cup.

3. Add noodles to boiling water and cook 3 to 4 minutes. Transfer to colander and drain.

4. Return pasta to stockpot. Add butter, season to taste with pepper and nutmeg, and toss to combine. Cover and keep warm.

5. Just before serving, toss again. Divide among plates and sprinkle with parsley or chives.

ADDED TOUCH

Gewürztztraminer is the primary flavoring for this refreshing sherbet. You will need an ice cream machine to make this dessert.

Gewürztraminer Sorbet

1 cup sugar
4 juice oranges
Medium-size lemon
1 bottle (750 ml) Gewürztraminer

1. For syrup, bring sugar and 1 cup water to a boil in small saucepan over high heat. Remove pan from heat and allow to cool to room temperature.

2. Squeeze enough oranges to measure 1 cup juice and enough lemon to measure 3 tablespoons.

3. Combine wine, syrup, orange juice, and lemon juice in medium-size bowl. Cover with plastic wrap and refrigerate until chilled.

4. Freeze mixture in an ice cream machine according to manufacturer's instructions.

5. Divide among parfait glasses and serve.

Acknowledgments

The Editors would like to thank the following for their courtesy in lending items for photography: *Cover:* servers—Gorham; platters, pots de crème—The Mediterranean Shop; linens—Pierre Deux. *Frontispiece:* tiles—Country Floors; baskets—Be Seated, Inc.; knife—Linda Campbell Franklin Collection; madeleine pan, copper sauté pan—Charles Lamalle; cutting board—Slotnick Collection. *Pages 16–17:* cloth—Wolfman-Gold & Good Company; pinch pot—Ann Ruthven; basket—Pottery Barn. *Pages 20–21:* tiles—Terra Design, Inc., Morristown, NJ; flatware—Frank McIntosh at Henri Bendel; plates—Columbus Avenue General Store; pitcher—Buffalo China. *Page 23:* flatware—Gorham; underplates—Dan Bleier. *Pages 26–27:* servers—Gorham; paella pan—Copco; dishes, tureen—Robert Haviland and C. Parlon. *Page 30:* flatware—Wallace Silversmiths; glasses—Gorham; cloth, napkin, dishes—Pierre Deux. *Page 33:* plate—Feu Follet; cloth—Steven Seebohm, Inc.; fork—Gorham. *Pages 36–37:* flatware—Wallace Silversmiths; dishes—Terrafirma. *Pages 40–41:* ladle—Wallace Silversmiths; napkin in basket—Pierre Deux; tureen, sauce boat, salad dishes—Richard Ginori. *Page 43:* flatware—Gorham; glass, dishes, napkin—Urban Outfitters; countertop—Formica® Brand Laminate by Formica Corp. *Pages 46–47:* flatware, glass—Gorham; dishes—Dan Bleier, courtesy of Creative Resources; napkin—Leacock & Company; tiles—Terra Design, Inc., Morristown, NJ. *Page 50:* dishes—Franciscan of Wedgwood; flatware—Gorham; tablecloth, napkin, glasses—Pierre Deux. *Page 53:* flatware—Gorham; cloth, napkin, dishes—Pottery Barn. *Pages 56–57:* flatware—Gorham; glasses—Ricci; tablecloth—Ad Hoc Softwares; dishes, napkins—Of All Things. *Page 60:* napkin—Ad Hoc Softwares; platters—Eigen Arts. *Page 62:* flatware—Wallace Silversmiths; plate—Buffalo China; paper—Four Hands Bindery. *Pages 64–65:* napkin—Fabindia; salad bowl—Feu Follet; knife—Linda Campbell Franklin Collection. *Page 68:* flatware, glass—Gorham; plate—Dan Levy. *Page 71:* cloth—Ad Hoc Softwares; platters—Phillip Mueller, NYC. *Pages 74–75:* flatware—Gorham; napkins—Leacock & Company; plates—Columbus Avenue General Store; cloth—Ad Hoc Softwares. *Page 78:* dishes, glasses—Conran's; copper casserole, ladle, pots de crème—Charles Lamalle. *Page 81:* flatware—Frank McIntosh at Henri Bendel; plate—Bennington Potteries. *Pages 84–85:* tiles—Terra Design, Inc., Morristown, NJ; bread basket—Terrafirma. *Page 88:* flatware—Gorham. *Pages 90–91:* flatware—Wallace Silversmiths; cloth—Leacock & Company. *Pages 94–95:* flatware—Gorham; dishes, cloth, napkins, glasses—Pierre Deux. *Page 98:* flatware—Ercuis; glasses—Baccarat; plates—Viking Glass from Columbus Avenue General Store; linens—Porthault. *Page 100:* mug—Conran's; napkin, dish, underplate—Wolfman-Gold & Good Company. *Kitchen equipment courtesy of:* White-Westinghouse, Commercial Aluminum Cookware Co., Robot-Coupe, Caloric, Kitchen-Aid, J.A. Henckels Zwillingswerk, Inc., Rubbermaid, Tappan, Litton Microwave Cooking, Schawbel Corp., Farberware.

Illustrations by Ray Skibinski
Production by Giga Communications

Index